GU00729106

THOMAS CROFTON CROKE
family which settled in Co
Elizabeth I, was born in C
had considerable talent as
from the age of fourteen m
excursions in the south of Ireland, sketching
and studying the character of the people. He
went to London in 1818 and worked as a
clerk in the Admiralty for thirty years.

The first volume of *Fairy Legends and
Traditions of the South of Ireland,* described
by him as 'the twilight tales of the
peasantry', appeared in 1825 and was an
immediate success, evoking praise from Sir
Walter Scott (who described him as
'little as a dwarf, keen-eyed as a hawk'),
Maria Edgeworth and Miss Mitford.
A second volume followed in 1828 and
they were translated into German by
the Brothers Grimm. He died in 1854
and is buried in Brompton Cemetery.

JAMES LYONS has a similar interest in the
folklore of County Cork and has undertaken
exhaustive research to track down old half-
forgotten stories.

Cover Illustration:
*Children Dancing at
the Crossroads*
by Trevor Fowler.
(National Gallery
of Ireland)

The Cork River

T. Crofton Croker and
James Lyons

Legends of Cork

ANVIL BOOKS

Duit-se a
DHONNCHA
a chroí na dílseachta,
nár loic riamh ar cháirde
ná ar chómh Éireannaigh.

First published in 1988 by
Anvil Books Limited
45 Palmerston Road, Dublin 6
New edition 1992

© James Lyons

ISBN 0 947962 67 0

Typesetting by Computertype Ltd.
Printed by Colour Books

Contents

Introduction

There is little in this book which has not been said before. Much of it has been said hundreds of times in different ways in different places. Most of it has been forgotten, even by the native inhabitants of the localities in which the stories are set.

The great antiquity of many of the stories presents difficulties in research. It is frequently found that the same story is set in two different periods of history involving, of necessity, different historical characters. Historical fact is interwoven with created fiction in such a way as to make it well-nigh impossible, within the limits of available source material, to extricate fact from fiction.

Nevertheless preparation of the legends has given me considerable satisfaction. For years I had known of the existence of the tales relating to The Lough of Cork, Carrig Cliodhna, the Giant's Stairs, and other Cork landmarks and I had some skimpy details. But my desire to make the material available to a wider readership gave me the necessary incentive to seek out the full stories. It was a pleasure to blow the dust off old tomes, and to present the legends to the young people of the new generation and to their parents.

It may be said that I have taken liberties with the stories. Indeed I have! But I have not interfered with fundamental details as contained in such sources, both in Irish and English, as were available to me. Sometimes I had to choose between one version and another, even between one detail and another, and in all such cases

I made the choice for no other reason than that it best suited my requirements at the moment. Indeed, throughout my reading and research it was borne home to me how greatly we are indebted to Corkman Crofton Croker for collecting so many of the traditional tales from the lips of his contemporaries over a hundred and fifty years ago. He, too, took liberties but he secured the legends for posterity.

In conclusion, I would like to thank the many people who helped me on my way: Miss M. Collins and the staff of the Cork City Library, and An t-Uasal Seán Ó Súilleabháin of Roinn Bhéaloideas Éireann, Baile Átha Cliath, for their help in uncovering sources of information; Mr. Jeremiah Twomey of Cork city who gave me details of the Matehy story as told to him by an uncle whose roots were deep in that countryside — details upon which I based my narrative; Mr. James Ryan of Watergrasshill — *Beannacht Dé la n-a anam dílis* — who, in answer to my rather vague enquiries, eventually led me to the Gobán Saor's Castle; and, particularly, Dan Nolan of Anvil Books, who lent me valuable material, and gave me advice and encouragement throughout.

To them, and to all whom I encountered on my wayfaring, and who gladly shared their knowledge with me, I say a sincere 'Thank You'.

JAMES LYONS
Cork,
June, 1988

JAMES LYONS

The Legend of The Lough

In olden times there was a king in Cork who lived in a rich palace on the southern edges of the marshes, beyond the hunched hill of Croatamore. He was a kind-hearted and generous king to his own, but cautious, and fearful lest any possessions would be wrested from him.

His palace lay within a sunny, shallow, saucer-shaped valley. It was a spread-eagled kind of place, with banqueting-hall, kitchens, dormitories, gaming-greens and stables loosely grouped around a great courtyard, and in the centre of the courtyard was a well. This was a wonderful well of clearest spring water, ice-cold in the warmest summer and brimming over even in times of prolonged drought. It was his most treasured possession and the wonder of his kingdom but, for all that, he shared it with the poor people of the district, who came to the courtyard daily to draw water for their household needs. All were welcome at the palace well.

In time, however, the king grew anxious as he watched so many people drawing water from his well, and soon the little worm of selfishness that was in him injected something of its poison into his mind, and he became fretful lest all the water be drained away. He thought about it and he thought about it, and the more he thought the more certain he became that soon the well would not be able to meet the demands being made of it.

He summoned his wife to him. 'Woman,' he said, 'I have been watching the people of the countryside coming with their pitchers and their churns to draw water from our well, and the notion is on me that maybe there is

9

not all that much water in it. What should I do?'

Now his wife, for all that she was a queen, was a wise and wily woman, as most women are, and she had not been married to him for thirty years without getting to understand the deviations of his mind.

'My advice to you is that you do nothing,' she told him tersely. 'Is it to be putting a fence around it you're thinking, to keep the poor people from getting a sup to drink? No good will come of it if you do.'

But the king was uneasy, as is sometimes the way with kings. Now in all their years together he had always acted on his wife's counsel; but not this time! Daily he grew more afraid that he would eventually be without water. In the end, he called in his chief mason and his blacksmith, ordered them to build a fine house around the well, and set a strong door with a special lock to guard it. Then he called in his goldsmith, and told him to fashion a richly ornamented goblet in which the water could be drawn. He slept soundly that night.

In time, when the house was built, and the thick double-plated door set in place and the strong lock fastened above the well, the king came to examine the work. He looked at the stout stonework, and he tested the great door, and he tried to wrench the shackle of the lock from its spindle with his strong hands. When he finished his inspection he was well pleased.

But misgiving breeds misgiving, and as he walked back across the courtyard, slow-footed, head bent, he thought to himself, 'Now, the well is secure, but can I be sure that my servants will not allow their friends from outside to sneak away water when they themselves unlock the door to draw water for the palace?' He walked all the way to the royal apartments, turning the thought over this way and that in his mind. And then he walked all the way back to the well.

He looked again at the door, and he thought of the clear water shining at the foot of the three stone steps inside and of the golden goblet in the great hall of the

Passage

palace. 'Only my daughter, the princess, may draw water from the well henceforth,' he decided. 'She, and she alone, shall have custody of key and goblet,' and, turning abruptly, he walked back to the palace, long-striding, with his full cape flowing freely from his broad, forward-thrusting shoulders.

So far so good, and that was not bad.

Time went by. The daughter of the house, the comely princess, alone took the gold goblet to the well, and the people of the locality had no other option but to draw water from the hillside springs. The king had found his own self-satisfied peace, having transferred a measure of his earlier uneasiness to his queen. She now had her own misgivings, though they were not those of the king. She had a premonition that subtle influences were already at work.

Some time after enclosing the well, the king held a banquet. From far and wide, from north and east and west, the chiefs and their minions came, and great indeed was the hosting in the shelter of Croatamore. The banquet-hall echoed to the sounds of song and laughter. The king was there, with his queen, presiding at the head of the long table, and the princess, on the king's right hand, played an age-old game, as she exchanged soft glances with the prince of a neighbouring kingdom.

Fresh food and the most mature of drinks were there, but nowhere in that great hall was a beaker of water to be seen. When, in the course of the feasting, one chief commented on this, the king was quick to respond. Had he not planned it so? 'Water?' asked the king. 'Why, if it's water you want, I have the finest that ever welled from the soil of Erin. Daughter, *a chroí* ... take the golden goblet to the well and bring water to our table.'

The princess showed signs of some confusion at being asked to do so menial a task in so noble a company, and the king, noting it, added, 'Your prince partner may accompany you, for the hour is late.' And so they went, prince and princess, into the courtyard.

It was a clear, balmy night, with a golden moon riding smoothly over the southern hills, and from those hills a warm breeze blew, rich with the scent of woodbine. They walked slowly and in silence across the courtyard toward the well, a comely couple, both of them sharing the one unspoken thought, and when by accident, or maybe by design, their shoulders touched they exchanged shy glances.

The princess paused a moment before unlocking the door of the house protecting the well, and the moon shone full on her face when she looked up into the prince's eyes. 'You wait here,' she commanded him, 'and I will hand the goblet to you.'

For a moment or two their eyes held and then, surprisingly, the girl rose on her toes ... and kissed him.

The great lock responded quietly to her touch, and the strong door swung outward smoothly on its greased hinges. Inside, the water sparkled golden under the moonlight which now splayed across its surface, and the gold goblet in her hands was no more golden than that golden light. She stood quietly at the head of the steps. It seemed to her that this place had taken on a new character by night. The steps seemed steeper, the water deeper, the atmosphere alien and threatening. She herself felt strangely subdued and ill-at-ease.

She descended the three steps slowly and paused again, looking down into the well. Then she sighed, sadly, wearily, resignedly one might be tempted to say, and she stooped, as a woman stoops, with grace and dignity, and dipped the golden cup. The water gurgled into it, ringing like so many tiny bells, and it became heavy — heavier than she had ever known it, as though it were being pulled from her from below.

'Prince!' she called urgently to her companion outside, and turned her head to look through the open door.

That quick movement upset her balance and she slipped, but it seemed not so much that she fell into the well as that the water leaped to meet her. It surged upward like a geyser so quickly that it caught the prince in the doorway, hurling him back into the courtyard, and in a very short time, even before he could reach the banqueting-hall with a warning, it had begun to flow into the ground-floor apartments of the palace, swallowing up the feasting company.

The water was now coming in an uncontrollable flood, and strong torrents began to pour through shattered gates and window-opes into the shallow valley-lands beyond until several hundred acres of green pasture had been submerged, and all signs of the royal buildings had disappeared. Two swans came flying in over the marshlands of the Lee estuary from the east, and planed down to settle on the shimmering moon-bright water. Then, and only then, did the spring subside, leaving behind a new lake in a tranquil land.

Many centuries later Saint Finbarr founded his monastery on a rocky plateau nearby, and a city grew and prospered along the banks of the Lee river until, spreading out gradually in all directions, it crept over and far beyond the hill of Croatamore. There, in the middle of modern housing estates, *Loch na bhFearnóg* — The Lough — remains to this day. The swans still grace its waters, and the small boys of Cork fish for roach and thorneens from its shallow shorelands. But no one has ever laid eyes on the king, the princess, nor any of that noble company.

Nevertheless, on moonlight nights in summer when a warm wind blows off the southern hills and the air is sweet with the scent of woodbine, a keen ear may still pick up the sound of song and laughter issuing from beneath the water. For those who were submerged so long ago live on. The great banquet continues still, and is destined to continue until someone, sometime, in some surprising way, recovers the golden goblet lost by the lovely princess in olden days.

T. CROFTON CROKER

The Headless Horseman

'God speed you, and a safe journey this night to you, Charley,' the master of the little *shebeen* house at Ballyhooley called after his old friend and good customer, Charley Culnane, who had, at last, turned his face homewards with the prospect of as dreary a ride on as dark a night as ever fell upon the Blackwater along whose banks he was about to journey.

Charley knew the country well, and he was as bold a rider as any Mallow boy that rattled a four-year-old upon Drumrue racecourse. He had gone to Fermoy in the morning, both to buy some ingredients required for the Christmas dinner by his wife and to gratify his own vanity by having new reins fitted to his snaffle; he intended showing off the mare at the approaching St. Stephen's Day hunt.

Charley did not leave Fermoy until late, for in all the appointments connected with hunting, riding, leaping, and in whatever was connected with the old mare, Charley was the devil to please. Why else would he have gone such a distance for a snaffle bridle? Mallow was full twelve miles nearer Charley's farm at Carrick than was Fermoy, but he had quarrelled with all the Mallow saddlers and no one could content him but honest Michael Twomey of Fermoy, who used to assert that he could stitch a saddle better than the lord-lieutenant.

The delay in Fermoy meant that Charley could not pay so long a visit as he had at first intended to his old friend and gossip, Con Buckley of the *Harp of Erin,* but Con knew the value of time and insisted upon Charley making good use of what he had to spare.

'I won't bother you waiting for water, Charley, because I think you'll have enough of that same before you get home. So drink your liquor, man. It's as good as ever a gentleman tasted.'

Charley, nothing loth, drank success to Con, and success to the *Harp of Erin* and to their better acquaintance, and so on, from the bottom of his soul, until the bottom of the bottle reminded him that Carrick was at the bottom of the hill on the other side of Castletownroche, and that he had got no further on his journey than Ballyhooley. Catching hold of his oil-skin hat, therefore, he bolted from his friend's hospitality, darted to the stable, tightened his girths, and put the old mare into a canter towards home.

The road from Ballyhooley to Carrick follows pretty nearly the course of the Blackwater, occasionally diverging from the river and passing through rather wild scenery. Charley cantered on gaily, regardless of the rain which, as his friend Con had anticipated, now fell in torrents. Though the visit to the *Harp of Erin* had a little increased the natural complacency of his mind, the drenching of the new snaffle reins began to disturb him. Then followed a train of more anxious thoughts for, in an hour of good fellowship when his heart was warm and his head not over-cool, he had backed the old mare against Mr. Jepson's bay filly Desdemona for a neat hundred, and he now felt sore misgivings as to the prudence of the match.

The old mare had reduced her canter to a trot at the bottom of Kilcummer Hill, and was now passing the old walls that belonged in former times to the Templars. The silent gloom of the place was broken only by the heavy rain which splashed and pattered on the gravestones, and Charlie looked up at the sky to see if there was, among the clouds, any hope of mercy for his new snaffle reins.

No sooner had he lowered his eyes than his attention

was arrested by an object so extraordinary as almost led him to doubt the evidence of his senses. The head of a white horse, with short cropped ears, large open nostrils and immense eyes, seemed to be beside him. No connection with body, legs or rider could be traced as the head advanced!

Charley's old mare, too, was moved at this unnatural sight and, snorting violently, increased her trot up the hill. The head moved forward, and passed them by.

Charley, still following it with astonished gaze, was suddenly conscious of some other being at his side. He turned to examine what was so sociably jogging beside him. A figure, whose height he computed to be at least eight feet, was seated on the body and legs of a white horse full eighteen hands and a half high.

After the first feeling of astonishment, the attention of Charley was naturally directed first to this extraordinary horse's body and, having examined it with the eye of a connoisseur, he then turned his attention to the human figure, who had so far remained perfectly mute. He tried to catch a sight of his companion's face, but he could see nothing beyond the top of the collar of the figure's coat — a scarlet single-breasted hunting-frock, having a waist of a very old-fashioned cut reaching to the saddle, with two huge shining buttons behind.

'I ought to be able to see further than the top of his collar,' thought Charley, 'although he is mounted on such a high horse. Unless Con's whiskey has blinded me entirely!'

However, see further he could not and, after straining his eyes for a considerable time to no purpose, he exclaimed with pure vexation, 'By the big bridge of Mallow, it is no head at all he has!'

'Look again, Charley Culnane,' said a hoarse voice that seemed to proceed from under the right arm of the figure.

Charley did look again, and now in the proper place, for under the aforesaid right arm he clearly saw the head from which the voice had proceeded. No speck of colour enlivened the ashy paleness of the depressed features, and the skin lay stretched over the unearthly surface, almost like the parchment head of a drum. Two fiery eyes flashed like meteors upon Charley, and the mouth peeped forth from under a profusion of black lustreless locks.

Charley, although a lad of proverbial courage in the county of Cork, could not but feel his nerves a little shaken by this unexpected visit from the headless horseman of whom he had often heard tell.

Meanwhile, the cropped-eared head of the gigantic horse moved steadily forward, always keeping about six to eight yards in advance. The headless horseman, unaided by whip or spur, and disdaining the use of stirrups which dangled uselessly from the saddle, followed at a trot by Charley's side. The ground shook under the weight of its supernatural burden, and the water in the pools was agitated into waves as he trotted by them. The deadly silence of the night was broken only by the fearful clattering of hoofs and the distant sound of thunder which rumbled above the mystic hill of *Cecanne a Mona Finnea.*

Charley, who was naturally a merry-hearted and rather talkative fellow, had up to now felt tongue-tied by apprehension, but finding his companion showed no evil disposition towards him, and having become somewhat more reconciled to the Patagonian dimensions of the horseman and his headless steed, he plucked up all his courage, and addressed the stranger.

'To be sure, that's a brave horse your honour rides,' he said.

'You may say that with your own ugly mouth,' growled the head.

'Maybe your honour would be thinking of riding him across the country?' Charley continued.

'Will you try me, Charley?' said the head, with an inexpressible look of ghastly delight.

'Faith, and that's what I'd like to do,' responded Charley, 'only I'm afraid, the night being so dark, of laming the old mare, and I've every halfpenny of a hundred pounds on her heels.'

That reservation apart, Charley's courage was nothing dashed at the headless horseman's proposal. There never was a steeplechase nor a fox-hunt nor any riding or leaping in the country, that Charley Culnane was not at it, and foremost in it.

'Will you take my word for the safety of your mare?' said the man who carried his head so snugly under his right arm.

'Done!' said Charley, and away they started, helter-skelter over everything, ditch and wall. The old mare never went in such style, even in broad daylight, and Charley had just the start of his companion when the hoarse voice called out, 'Charley Culnane! Charley, man, stop for your life! Stop!'

Charley pulled up hard. 'Ay,' thought he, 'you may beat me by the head, because yours always goes so much before you, but if the bet was neck and neck and that's

19

the go between the old mare and Desdemona — I'd win it hollow!'

It seemed as if the stranger was well aware of what was passing in Charley's mind, for he suddenly broke out, 'Charley Culnane, you have a stout soul in you and are every inch of you a good rider — I've tried you and I ought to know — and that's the sort of man for my money. A hundred years it is since my horse and I broke our necks at the bottom of Kilcummer Hill, and ever since I have been trying to get a man that dared to ride with me and never found one before. Keep, as you have always done, at the tail of the hounds, never baulk a ditch nor turn away from a stone wall, and the headless horseman will never desert you nor the old mare.'

Charley, in amazement, looked toward the stranger's right arm, for the purpose of seeing in his face whether or not he was in earnest, but behold! The head was snugly lodged in the huge pocket of the horseman's scarlet hunting-coat. The horse's head had ascended perpendicularly above them, and his extraordinary companion, rising quickly after his *avant courier,* vanished from the astonished gaze of Charley Culnane.

Charley, as may be supposed, was lost in wonder, delight, and perplexity. The pelting rain, the wife's pudding, the new snaffle, even the match against squire Jepson, all were forgotten. Nothing could he think of, nothing could he talk of, but the headless horseman. He told it, as soon as he got home, to Judy. He told it the following morning to all the neighbours. He told it to the hunt on St. Stephen's Day. But what provoked him, after all the pains he took in describing the head, the horse and the man, was that one and all attributed the creation of the headless horseman to his friend Con Buckley's whiskey.

Nevertheless, Charley's old mare did beat Mr. Jepson's bay filly Desdemona and Charley pocketed his cool hundred pounds.

T. CROFTON CROKER

The Death-Coach

TIS midnight! — how gloomy and dark!
  By Jupiter, there's not a star!—
'Tis fearful! — 'tis awful! — and, hark!
  What sound is that comes from afar?

Still rolling and rumbling, that sound
  Making nearer and nearer approach;
Do I tremble, or is it the ground? —
  Lord, save us! — what is it? — a coach! —

A coach! but that coach has no head;
  And the horses are headless as it;
Of the driver the same may be said,
  And the passengers inside who sit.

See the wheels! how they fly o'er the stones!
  And whirl, as the whip it goes crack:
Their spokes are of dead men's thigh-bones,
  And the pole is the spine of the back!

The hammercloth, shabby display,
  Is a pall rather mildew'd by damps;
And to light this strange coach on its way,
  Two hollow skulls hang up for lamps!

From the gloom of Rathcooney churchyard,
  They dash down the hill of Glanmire;
Pass Lota in gallop as hard
  As if horses were never to tire!

With people thus headless 'tis fun
    To drive in such furious career;
Since *headlong* their horses can't run,
    Nor coachman be *heady* from beer.

Very steep is the Tivoli lane,
    But up-hill to them is as down;
Nor the charms of Woodhill can detain
    These Dullahans rushing to town.

Could they feel as I've felt — in a song —
    A spell that forbade them depart;
They'd a lingering visit prolong,
    And after their head lose their heart!

No matter! — 'tis past twelve o'clock;
    Through the streets they sweep on like the wind,
And, taking the road to Blackrock,
    Cork city is soon left behind.

Should they hurry thus reckless along
    To supper instead of to bed,
The landlord will surely be wrong
    If he charge it at so much a head!

Yet mine host may suppose them too poor
    To bring to his wealth an increase;
As till now, all who drove to his door,
    Possess'd at least *one crown* apiece.

Up the Deadwoman's hill they are roll'd;
    Boreenmannah is quite out of sight;
Ballintemple they reach, and behold!
    At its churchyard they stop and alight.

'Who's there?' said a voice from the ground;
    'We've no room, for the place is quite full.'
'Oh, room must be speedily found,
    For we come from the parish of Skull.

'Though Murphys and Crowleys appear
  On headstones of deep-letter'd pride;
Though Scannels and Murleys lie here,
  Fitzgeralds and Toomies beside;

'Yet here for the night we lie down,
  To-morrow we speed on the gale;
For having no heads of our own,
  We seek the Old Head of Kinsale.'

T. CROFTON CROKER

Barry of Cairn Thierna

Many, many years ago it happened that a regiment of foot soldiers was en route from Dublin to Cork. During the march, one company left Cahir in the morning, passed through Mitchelstown, tramped across the Kilworth mountains and late of an October evening, tired and hungry, reached Fermoy, the last stage but one of their journey. There were no barracks there then to receive them, and so every voice was raised, calling to the gaping villagers for the name and residence of the billet-master.

Mr. Considine, the billet-master, was a person of great importance in Fermoy. He was of portly build, and of a grave and slow movement suited to his stature. Three inches of fair linen were at all times visible between his waistband and waistcoat. His breeches pockets were never buttoned and, scorning to conceal the bull-like proportions of his chest and neck, his collar was generally open, as he wore no cravat. A flaxen bob-wig commonly sat fairly on his head and squarely on his forehead, and an ex-officio pen was stuck behind his ear. Such was Mr. Considine, billet-master-general, barony sub-constable and deputy-clerk of the sessions, who was now just getting near the end of his eighth tumbler in company with the proctor.

Mr. Considine's own pen, and that of his son Tom, were soon full of employment. The officers were sent to the inn. The sergeants, corporals, and lesser ranks were billeted on those who were on indifferent terms with him for, like a worthy man, he leaned as lightly as he could on his friends.

The soldiers had nearly all departed for their quarters when one poor fellow, who had fallen asleep leaning on his musket against the wall, was awakened by the silence and, starting up, he went over to the table at which Mr. Considine was seated, hoping his worship would give him a good billet.

'A good billet, my lad?' said the billet-master-general, barony sub-constable and deputy-clerk of the sessions. 'That you shall have, and in the biggest house in the place. Do you hear, Tom! Make out a billet for this man upon Mr. Barry of Cairn Thierna.'

'On Mr. Barry of Cairn Thierna!' said Tom with surprise.

'Yes! On Mr. Barry of Cairn Thierna — the great Barry!' replied his father, giving a nod and closing his right eye slowly with a semi-drunken wink. 'Is he not said to keep the grandest house in this part of the country? Or stay, Tom! Just hand me over the paper and I'll write the billet myself.'

The billet was made out accordingly, and the weary grenadier received it with becoming gratitude and thanks. Taking up his knapsack and firelock he left the office, and Mr. Considine waddled back to the proctor to chuckle over the trick he had played on the soldier, and to laugh at the idea of the forthcoming search after Barry of Cairn Thierna's house.

Barry was one of the chieftains who lorded it over the barony of Barrymore in olden days. Legend associated him with the mountain of Cairn Thierna where he was known to live in great state, and was often seen by the belated traveller.

Mr. Considine had informed the soldier that Mr. Barry lived a little way out of town on the Cork road, so the poor fellow trudged along for some time, with eyes right and eyes left, looking for the great house. But nothing could he see only the dark mountain of Cairn Thierna before him, and an odd cabin or two on the roadside. At last he met a man of whom he asked the way.

'Mr. Barry's?' said the man. 'What Barry do you want?'

'I can't say exactly,' returned the soldier. 'Mr. What's-his-name, the billet-master, has given me the direction of my billet, but he said it was a large house and I think he called him the great Mr. Barry.'

'Why, sure, it wouldn't be the great Barry of Cairn Thierna you are asking about?'

'Ay,' said the soldier, 'Cairn Thierna — that's the very place. Can you tell me where it is?'

'Cairn Thierna,' repeated the man. 'Barry of Cairn Thierna? It's the first time in all my born days that ever I heard of a soldier being billeted on Barry of Cairn Thierna. 'Tis surely a queer thing for old Dick Considine to be after sending you there. Anyway, I'll show you the way and welcome. You see that big mountain before you, that's Cairn Thierna. Go right to the top of it, up to the big heap of stones, and anyone will show you Mr. Barry's.'

The weary soldier gave a sigh as he walked forward toward the mountain. He had not proceeded far when he heard the clatter of a horse coming along the road after him, and turning his head around he saw a dark figure rapidly approaching him. A tall gentleman, richly dressed and mounted on a noble grey horse, was soon at his side. The rider pulled up, and the soldier repeated his inquiry after Mr. Barry's of Cairn Thierna.

'I'm Barry of Cairn Thierna,' said the gentleman. 'What is your business with me, friend?'

'I've got a billet on your house, sir,' replied the soldier, 'from the billet-master of Fermoy.'

'Have you, indeed?' said Barry. 'Well, it is not far off. Follow me, and you shall be well taken care of.'

He turned off the road and led the way up the steep side of the mountain, followed by the soldier who was astonished at seeing the horse proceed so easily where he could only scramble up with difficulty, hardly able to find or keep his footing. When they got to the top, there was a house sure enough, far more splendid than any in Fermoy. It was three stories high, with fine windows, and all lighted up within as if it was full of grand company. There was a hall door too, with a flight of stone steps before it, at which Mr. Barry dismounted. The door was opened to him by a servant man who took his horse round to the stable.

Mr. Barry invited the soldier in, and instead of sending him down to the kitchen, as any other gentleman would have done, brought him into the parlour.

'Ay,' said Mr. Barry, looking at him and smiling, 'I know Dick Considine well — he's a merry fellow, and has got some excellent cows on the Inch field of Carrickabrick. A sirloin of good beef is no bad thing for supper.'

Mr. Barry then called out to some of his attendants, and asked them to lay the cloth and make all ready. No sooner was this done than a smoking sirloin of beef was placed before them.

'Sit down now, my honest fellow,' said Mr. Barry, 'you must be hungry after your long day's march.'

The soldier, with a profusion of thanks for such hospitality, sat down and made an excellent supper. Then the boiling water was brought in, and a jug of whiskey-punch was made that there was no faulting.

They sat together a long time, talking over the punch, and the fire was so good and Mr. Barry himself had such fine converse about everything in the world, far or near, that the soldier never felt the night going over him. At last Mr. Barry stood up, saying it was a rule with him that every one in his house should be in bed by twelve o'clock. Then, pointing to a bundle which lay in one corner of the room, he said, 'Take that to bed with you. It's the hide of the cow which I had killed for your supper. Give it to the billet-master when you go back to Fermoy in the morning, and tell him that Barry of Cairn Thierna sent it to him. He will understand what it means, I promise you. So good-night, my brave fellow, I wish you a comfortable sleep, and every good

fortune, but I must be off and away out of this long before you are stirring.'

The soldier gratefully returned his host's good-night and good wishes, and went off to the room which was shown to him.

Next morning the sun awoke him. He was lying on the broad of his back, the skylark was singing over him in the beautiful blue sky and the bees were humming close to his ear among the heather. He rubbed his eyes. Nothing did he see but the clear sky with two or three morning clouds floating by. Mr. Barry's fine house and soft feather bed had melted into thin air, and he found himself stretched on the side of Cairn Thierna, buried in the heath, with the cow-hide which had been given to him rolled up under his head for a pillow.

'Well,' said he, 'this beats cock-fighting! Didn't I spend the pleasantest night I ever spent in my life with Mr. Barry last night? And what in the world has become of the house, and the hall door with the steps, and the very bed that was under me?'

He stood up. Not a vestige of a house or anything like one could he see, only the rude heap of stones on the top of the mountain. Way down below lay the Blackwater, with the little quiet village of Fermoy on its banks. Throwing the cow-hide over his shoulder he descended, not without some difficulty, the steep side of the mountain up which Mr. Barry and his horse had led him the preceding night with so much ease, pondering on what had befallen him.

When he reached Fermoy he went straight to Mr. Considine's house and asked to see him.

'Well, my good fellow,' said Mr.Considine, recognising at a glance the soldier, 'what sort of an entertainment did you meet with from Barry of Cairn Thierna?'

'The best treatment, sir,' replied the soldier, 'and well did he speak of you. He asked me to give you this cow-hide as a token to remember him.'

'Many thanks to Mr. Barry for his generosity,' said the billet-master, making a bow in mock solemnity. 'Many thanks, indeed, and a right good skin it is, wherever he got it.'

Mr. Considine had scarcely finished the sentence when he saw his cow-boy running up the street, shouting and crying aloud that the best cow in the Inch field was lost and gone, and nobody knew what had become of her, or could give the least tidings of her.

The soldier had flung the skin on the ground, and the cow-boy, looking at it, exclaimed, 'That is her hide, wherever she is! I'd take my bible oath to the two small white spots with the glossy black about them, and there's the very place where she rubbed hair off her shoulder last Martinmas.'

'There's no manner of doubt of it,' Mr. Considine admitted. 'It was Barry who killed my best cow, and all he has left me is the hide of the poor beast to comfort myself with. But it will be a warning to Dick Considine for the rest of his life never again to play off his tricks upon travellers.'

T. CROFTON CROKER

Dreaming Tim Jarvis

As everybody knows who knows Ballydehob, Timothy Jarvis was a decent, honest, quiet, hard-working man. He was thriving enough to be able to give his daughter Nelly a middling good fortune, and he would have been snug enough himself but that he loved the drop sometimes. However, he was seldom backward on rent day. His ground was never distrained but twice, and both times through a small bit of a mistake.

Now, it so happened that, being heavy in himself through the drink, Tim took to sleeping, and the sleep set him dreaming, and he dreamed all night, night after night, about crocks full of gold and precious stones. At last he dreamt that he found a mighty great crock of gold and silver — and where, do you think? Every step of the way upon London Bridge itself. Three times Tim dreamt the same thing, and at last he made up his mind to go over to London in Pat Mahoney's coaster — and so he did!

Well, he got there, and found the bridge without much difficulty. Every day he walked up and down looking for the crock of gold, but never did he find it.

One day, however, as he was looking over the bridge into the water a man, or something like a man, with great black whiskers and a black cloak that reached down to the ground, tapped him on the shoulder, and said, 'Tim Jarvis, do you see me?'

'Surely I do, sir,' said Tim, wondering that anybody should know him in the strange place.

'Tim,' said he, 'what is it brings you here to foreign

30

parts, so far away from your own cabin by the mine of grey copper at Ballydehob?'

'Indeed then,' said Tim, 'I've come to seek my fortune.'

'You're a fool for your pains, Tim, if that's all,' remarked the stranger in the black cloak. 'This is a big place to seek one's fortune in, to be sure, but it's not so easy to find it.'

'There's many a one like me comes here seeking their fortunes,' said Tim.

'True,' said the stranger.

'But,' continued Tim, looking up, 'the body and bones of the cause for myself leaving the wife, and Nelly, and the boys, is to look for a crock of gold that I'm told is lying somewhere hereabouts.'

'And who told you that, Tim?'

'Why then, sir, that's what I can't tell myself rightly ... only I dreamt it.'

'Ho, ho! Is that all, Tim?' said the stranger, laughing. 'I had a dream myself ... and I dreamed that I found a crock of gold in the fort field, on Jerry Driscoll's ground at Ballydehob. And, by the same token, the pit where it lay was close to a large furze bush all full of yellow blossom.'

Tim knew Jerry Driscoll's ground well. And moreover, he knew the fort field as well as he knew his own potato garden. He was certain, too, of the very furze bush at the north end of it. So, swearing a bitter big oath, he said, 'By all the crosses in a yard of check cloth, I always thought there was money in that same field!'

The moment he rapped out the oath the stranger disappeared, and Tim Jarvis, wondering at all that had happened him, made the best of his way back to Ireland. Nora had no very great welcome for her runaway husband — the dreaming blackguard! But he looked so cheerful and so happy after his long journey that she could not find it in her heart to be cross with him, and he managed to pacify her by two or three broad hints about a new cloak and pair of shoes, and decent clothes for Nelly to go to the pattern with her sweetheart, and brogues for the boys, and some corduroy for himself.

'It wasn't for nothing,' said Tim, 'I went to foreign parts all the ways, and you'll see what will come out of it ... mind my words.'

A few days afterwards Tim sold everything he had in the world — his cabin and his garden — and bought the fort field of Jerry Driscoll that had nothing in it but thistles and old stones and blackberry bushes. It was said to be the backbone of the world, picked by the devil, and all the world, as well it might, thought he was cracked.

The first night that Tim could summon courage to begin his work he walked off to the field with his spade on his shoulder, and away he dug all night by the side of the furze bush till he came to a big stone. He struck his spade against it, and he heard a hollow sound. But as the morning had begun to dawn, and the neighbours would be going out to their work Tim, not wishing to have the thing talked about, went home to the little hovel where Nora and the children were huddled together under a heap of straw.

It is impossible to describe the epithets and reproaches bestowed by the poor woman on her unlucky husband for bringing her into such a way, but as soon as night came again Tim stood beside the furze bush, spade in hand. The moment he jumped down into the pit he heard a strange rumbling noise under him. Putting his ear against the stone he listened, and overheard a discourse that made the hair on his head stand up like bulrushes and every limb tremble.

'How shall we bother Tim?' said one voice.

'Take him to the mountain, to be sure, and make him a toothful for the old serpent; 'tis long since he had a good meal,' said another voice.

'No,' said a third voice, 'plunge him in the bog, neck and heels.'

32

Tim was a dead man, barring the breath!

'Stop,' said a fourth, but Tim heard no more. In about an hour he came to, and he crept home to Nora.

When the next night arrived the hopes of the crock of gold got the better of his fears, and taking care to arm himself with a bottle of *potheen* away he went to the field.

Jumping into the pit he took a little sup from the bottle to keep his heart up. He then took a big one and, with a desperate heave, he wrenched up the stone. All at once up rushed a blast of wind, wild and fierce, and down fell Tim — down, down, down, until he thumped upon what seemed to be a floor of sharp pins which made him bellow out in earnest. Then he heard a whisk and a hurrah, and instantly voices beyond number cried out, 'Welcome, Tim Jarvis, dear, welcome down here!'

Tim's teeth chattered like magpies with the fright, but he could see nothing because the place was so dark and so lonesome in itself for want of light. Then something pulled Tim by the hair of his head and dragged him away faster than the wind. Then there was a whispering and a great hugger-mugger, and at last a pretty little bit of a voice said, 'Shut your eyes and you'll see, Tim.'

'By my word, then,' said Tim, 'that is the queer way of seeing. But I'm not the man to gainsay you, so I'll do as you bid me, anyhow.'

Presently he felt a small warm hand rubbed over his eyes with an ointment, and in the next minute he saw himself in the middle of thousands of little men and women who were pelting one another with golden guineas and lily-white thirteens. The finest dressed and the biggest of them, and none of them was half as high as his brogue, went up to him and said, 'Tim Jarvis, because you are a decent, honest, quiet, civil, well-spoken man, and know how to behave yourself in strange company, we've altered our minds about you, and we'll find a neighbour of yours that will do just as well to give to the old serpent.'

'Oh, then, long life to you, sir,' said Tim, 'and there's no doubt of that.'

'But what will you say, Tim, if we fill your pockets with these yellow boys? What will you say, Tim, and what will you do with them?'

'I'll not be able to say my prayers for one month with thanking you . . . and indeed I've enough to do with them. I'd make a grand lady, you see, at once of Nora . . . she has been a good wife to me. We'll have a nice bit of pork for dinner . . . and maybe I'd have a glass, or maybe two glasses, or sometimes — if 'twas with a friend or acquaintance or gossip — maybe three glasses every day . . . and I'd build a new cabin . . . and I'd have a fresh egg every morning for my breakfast . . . and I'd snap my fingers at the squire . . . and I'd have a new plough . . . and Nora should have a new cloak . . . and the boys should have shoes and stockings as well as Biddy Leary's brats — that's my sister that was! And I'd have a cow, and a beautiful coat with shining buttons, and a horse to ride, or maybe two. I'd have everything in life, good or bad, that is to be got for love or money . . . hurrah-whoop! . . . and that's what I'd do.'

'Take care, Tim,' said the little fellow. 'Your money would go faster than it came, with your hurrah-whoop.'

But Tim heeded not this speech. Heaps of gold were around him, and he filled and filled away, as hard as he could, his coat and his waistcoat and his breeches pockets. And he thought himself very clever because he stuffed some of the guineas in his brogues. When the little people perceived this they cried out, 'Go home, Tim Jarvis, go home, and think yourself a lucky man.'

'I hope, gentlemen,' said he, 'we won't part for good and all. Maybe ye'll ask me to see you again, and to give you a fair and square account of what I've done with your money.'

To this there was no answer, only another shout, 'Go home, Tim Jarvis, go home. Fair play is a jewel, but shut your eyes or you'll never see the light of day again.'

Tim shut his eyes, knowing now that was the way to see clearly, and away he was whisked as before till he stopped all of a sudden. He rubbed his eyes with his two thumbs, and where was he but in the very pit in the field that was Jerry Driscoll's and his wife Nora above him with a big stick ready to beat him. Tim roared out to the woman to leave the life in him, and he put his hands in his pockets to show her the gold. But he pulled out nothing only a handful of small stones mixed with yellow furze blossoms. The bush was under him, and the great flagstone that he had wrenched up, as he thought, was lying by his side. The whiskey bottle was drained to the last drop, and the pit was just as his spade had made it.

Tim Jarvis, vexed, disappointed and almost heart-broken, followed his wife home and, strange to say, from that night he left off drinking and dreaming and delving in bog-holes and rooting in old caves. He took again to his hard-working habits, and he was soon able to buy back his little cabin and former potato garden, and he got as much enjoyment from them as if he had purchased them with fairy gold.

JAMES LYONS

The Forsaken Grave on Shournaghside

Blarney village nestles on a green plain ringed around with rounded green hills that carry roistering rivers down from the foothills of the Boggeragh and Nagles Mountains. The houses front a green quadrangle edged with trees, and three roads enter the village at three corners of the square — from the south-east, the north-east, and the north-west. The castle, the mecca to which most visitors to Blarney gravitate, stands in its own grounds off the south-west corner.

But the lore and legend of Blarney do not end with a stone in the battlements of the old castle. History is written in bold characters across the landscape.

The road which runs from the north-western corner of the village hems the hills on the northern edges of the plain, but an off-shoot climbs and winds upward through deciduous woods, levelling off eventually on a long ridge that gives an extensive prospect of shallow valleys and distant mountains. Standing stones, fairy forts, and druidical remains abound upon these uplands and the misty grey lowlands themselves appear vaguely mystical. Downhill, and to the left, the Shournagh River hastens southward from Donoughmore to join the sister River Martin in the green lands of Blarney.

The road traverses the spine of the ridge for a time, then descends gradually and follows the course of the Lyredane stream, which is a tributary to the Shournagh, to Fox's Bridge. Uphill again, across the Shournagh, Matehy church stands overlooking the valley, and Matehy graveyard sleeps quietly on the hilltop.

Half way along that road between Blarney and Matehy is an old ring fort called *Lios na Reatha* and nearby, lower down on the hill above the Shournagh, is a place called Loughane. This is reputed to be the site of an ancient graveyard, which had been in use from the early days of Christianity in Ireland right up to the Penal Days. But it would be a waste of time to look for traces of that burial ground today; all that is left of it is a vague impression of a single marked grave — or so they say.

The soldiers were in gay mood that grey morning a couple of centuries ago when their officer led them out from barracks in pursuit of their favourite game. The mists were heavy on the hills, the rivers were in full flood after a month of rainy weather, and priest-hunting was just the occupation to boost the sagging morale of the men. A round dozen of them, they cantered across the old bridge at Inniscarra and followed the road through the woods, uphill and over, on their way to Cloghroe. It was chancy country to be travelling in on a mission of oppression and many the slights, many the jeers they suffered on the way. They staved off attackers under the Ardrum woods and, as the day wore on and the miles lengthened with not one priest's head lopped, the men's gaiety turned sour.

The Mass Rock near Cloghroe was deserted, and so they continued across the hills out of the valley of the Owenagearagh River into the Shournagh Valley. They crossed the river, and criss-crossed the moorland upland from the water. Here the mist was heavy on the marshes, and it was only by chance that they slipped unnoticed past the scouts and stumbled on a priest celebrating Mass before an unsuspecting congregation. The soldiers whooped. Bodily discomfort, ill humour and frayed tempers had been their travelling companions for too long that day, and now they unloosed the fury of their frustration. Spurring their horses into the crowd they flailed to left and right, and the officer himself moved quickly for the kill. The priest's head was his and, spiking it on his sword's point, he led his men triumphantly from the place.

Downhill again they cantered, displaying their prize as a gory warning to the Catholic community. Misjudging now the ford across the Shournagh the officer led the way into deep water. The horse shied, threw its rider and scrambled to the bank, but the officer fell headlong into the swollen river and smashed his skull on a submerged rock. His soldiers recovered the battered corpse at the shallows farther downstream. They consulted together, wondering how best to handle the situation. One of the soldiers, raising his eyes to the hillside, caught a glimpse of the old graveyard at Loughane, and there and then it was agreed that they should bury the officer's body there. And so they did.

They raided a nearby farmyard, and stole shovel and spade, and set to work digging the grave in a corner of the burial-ground. Sullen eyes watched them from hidden places, but no one dared to interfere with them. They watched the body being dropped into the pit, and saw the last shovelful of clay being hurled roughly over the grave. When the soldiers had eventually gone away over the hill they came out furtively to whisper among themselves of the dire things they had witnessed that day. Their first concern was for their murdered priest, and they talked of him long into the night. Eventually they did get to bed but no one in the parish, living or dead, had a restful night that night.

Some time before dawn a great commotion arose over the whole area of Loughane graveyard. At first the surface moved in some sort of convulsion. Then headstones tottered and swayed. Then the skeletons of the dead began to climb out of the ground, and the whole place was crowded to the hedges. There was a great chatter and consultation, and then, as if to a specific order, the whole community of the dead hoisted their tombstones and moved downhill to cross the Shournagh.

And for nearly a mile
Over meadow and bawn,
Over hedges and ditches,
And garden and lawn,
Rushed a skeleton host
With their bones shining white,
Ghastly and grim
In the mountain's pale light.
Some were dancing in circles
In elfin delight,
Some were struggling in shrouds
That encumbered their flight,
Some were bearing their tombstones
Like trophies of state,
And each skeleton breast
Bore its own coffin plate

The dawn was already glimmering in the east so they made haste, and in the hurry one or two of the tombstones fell from bony hands into the river. Up the hill they scrambled, and as they reached the top of the ridge a cock crew in a farm below them. They pitched their stones in the open ground, and hurriedly slid under the green sod as smoothly as if it had been into bed. And that's where the people found them in the morning, settled in on the site where Matehy graveyard lies to day.

Matehy! The name itself confirms the story — the plain of the fleeing — the flight from the priest-slayer. For over there at Loughane the one lonely grave had been left behind as a grim reminder of a bloody deed, and so it remains to the present day.

T. CROFTON CROKER

The Priest's Supper

It is·said by those who ought to understand such things that the little people, or fairies, are some of the angels who were turned out of heaven and landed on their feet in this world, while the rest of their companions, who had heavier sins to sink them, were sent down further to a worse place.

Be that as it may, there was a merry troop of fairies dancing and playing all manner of wild pranks on a bright moonlight evening towards the end of September, not far distant from the village of Inchigeela in West Cork. On a nice green sod by the river's side the little fellows were dancing in a ring as gaily as could be, with their red caps wagging about at every bound, and so spritely were they that the lobes of dew were not disturbed by their capering. They gambolled and cavorted, spinning round and round, twirling and bobbing and diving, and going through all manner of figures until one of them chirped out,

> *Cease, cease with your drumming,*
> *Here's an end to our mumming;*
> *By my smell*
> *I can tell*
> *A priest this way is coming*

And away they scampered as hard as they could. Some of them concealed themselves under the green leaves of the foxgloves where, if their little red caps should happen to peep out, they would look like the flowers' crimson bells. Others hid at the shady side of stones and brambles, or under the bank of the river in holes and crannies of one kind or another.

The fairy speaker had not been mistaken, for along the road, which was in view of the river, came Father Horrigan on his pony, thinking to himself that as it was so late he would put up at the first cabin he came to. Accordingly, he stopped at the home of Dermot O'Leary, lifted the latch, and entered with, 'My blessing on all here.'

Father Horrigan was a welcome guest wherever he went, for no man was more affable or better beloved in the county, and Dermot was perturbed that he had nothing more tasty to offer the priest for supper than the potatoes which his wife had boiling over the fire. He thought of the net he had set up in the river, but as it had been there only a short time he knew the chances were against finding a fish in it.

Nevertheless he went down to the river side. There, to his surprise, he found as fine a salmon as had ever been netted in the River Lee, but as he was going to take it out the net was pulled from him and away went the salmon, swimming as peacefully as if nothing had happened.

Dermot looked sorrowfully at the wake which the fish had left upon the water, shining like a line of silver in the moonlight, and with an angry motion of his right hand and a strong stamp of his foot, gave vent to his feelings. 'Bad luck to you for a salmon,' he shouted after it across the water. ''Twas the devil himself, for sure, helped you to escape.'

'That's not true,' piped one of the little people, coming out from hiding with the whole throng of companions at his heels. 'There was only a dozen and a half of us pulling against you. And make yourself noways uneasy about the priest's supper for, if you will go back and ask him one question from us, there will be as fine a supper as ever he tasted spread out on the table before him in less than no time.'

41

Dermot gazed open-mouthed at the tiny speaker, but as soon as he recovered his wits he answered in a tone of determination.

'I'll have nothing at all to do with you. I'm much obliged to you, but I know better than to sell myself to you, or the like of you, for a supper. And, furthermore, I know Father Horrigan wouldn't wish it, supper or no supper.'

The little speaker continued patiently, 'Will you just ask the priest one civil question for us?'

Dermot considered that proposition for some time, and then decided that no one could come to harm by asking a civil question.

'Very well, so,' he agreed, 'but, mind you, I'll have nothing at all to do with your supper.'

'Then,' said the little speaker, while the rest came crowding after him from all directions, 'go and ask Father Horrigan to tell us whether our souls will be saved at the Last Day like the souls of good Christians, and if you wish us well bring us back word what he says without delay.'

Dermot hurried home and found that his wife had already served a plate of steaming hot potatoes to the priest.

'Excuse me, Father,' Dermot said, after some hesitation, 'may I make so bold as to ask you one question?'

'And what may that be?' Father Horrigan asked.

'Could you tell me, Father, if the souls of the little people are to be saved at the Last Day?'

The priest fixed his steadfast eyes on him, and his tone was stern when he questioned him.

'Who bade you ask me that question, Dermot Leary?'

'God's truth, Father,' Dermot blurted out, ''twas the good people themselves sent me to ask the question. There are thousands of them down on the bank of the river waiting for me to go back with the answer.'

'Go back by all means,' said the priest, 'and tell them that if they want to know they must come here to me

42

themselves, and I'll answer that, or any other question they are pleased to ask, with the greatest pleasure in life.'

Dermot accordingly returned to the fairies, who came swarming around him to hear what the priest had said in reply, and Dermot spoke out among them like the bold man he was. But, when they heard that they must go to the priest, away they fled, some here and more there, some this way and more that, whisking by poor Dermot so fast and in such numbers that he was quite bewildered.

When he came to himself, which was not for a long time, he went back to his cabin and ate dry potatoes along with Father Horrigan, and he could not help thinking it a mighty hard case that the priest, whose words had the power to banish the fairies at such a rate, should have been deprived of that fine salmon in such a manner.

JAMES LYONS

A Legend of Kilcrea Friary

When the southern road from Cork to Macroom leaves
the Lee Valley it follows the course of another river,
the South Bride, that rises in the hills south-west of
Crookstown and joins the Lee at Inniscarra. Many
byroads lead off into the countryside north and south,
and each of them is worth investigation.

About ten miles west from the city, near the village
of Farran, one such road hairpins into the south-east.
It is an insignificant *bohereen,* threading its way between
gently rolling fields, but it holds the mellowing light of
the sun at evening and the blossomy hedges ring with
the songs of birds. It hems the skirts of small rounded
hills, shelters under beech trees that grow by the way
and, sighting the sparkle of running water, it rushes down
a slope to the river's edge.

Less than half a mile from the main highway an old
bridge of little arches spans the stream, and behind it,
across the water, an ancient ruin sprawls on level ground.

One evening in May I stood upon the bridge looking
at that ruin. A short distance away, approaching from
the west, a farm-cart rattled lazily on the rutted road,
its sound in harmony with the murmur of the water
over stones and the sighing of air in the streamside grasses.
An oldish man held the reins, his hat atilt over his eyes
to shield them from the sun. He stopped on the crown
of the bridge.

'God be with you, *a mhic,'* he greeted me, using the
Irish idiom, 'a grand day, and 'twill hold long as the
wind is in the east.'

44

When I turned to acknowledge his greeting he was looking out over my head at the ruin. 'Ah, the old days,' he said, a note of sadness in his voice. 'Wouldn't the peace and the loneliness of the place hold you?'

Then he surprised me by raising his voice a tone and reciting, with obvious feeling, Denis Florence MacCarthy's proud lines:

MacCaura, the pride of thy House is gone by,
But its name cannot fade and its fame cannot die

'I'm a MacCarthy myself,' he finished by way of explanation and, silent for a moment, he rested thoughtful eyes upon the ruin. 'There's a long, long history attached to this place,' he continued. '*Kilcrea* — the church of Saint Cera. She had a convent here in the time of the saints and scholars, but this ruin you're looking at was a foundation of the Franciscan Friars, built for them by Cormac Láidir MacCarthy of Blarney,

and dedicated to Saint Brigid. He's buried in there with many of his descendants. Do you remember the poem you learned at school about Art O'Leary? Well, Art's in there too. And Bishop O'Herlihy who attended the Council of Trent. A brave man that! He spent three years in the Tower of London, and did time in Dublin Castle as well.'

He paused again, but not for long. 'Here's something you may not have heard,' he continued. 'In olden times there was a labouring man working here — a fellow by the name of Donagh O'Dea. He was a sort of general factotem about the monastery grounds, keeping tally of all stock passing in and out of the place. His wife, Mary, did her share of the work, too, and to give them their due they were an honest enough pair, and hardworking. Of course, 'twas a nice situation for them. They were fine and comfortable with their own little house down by the gates.

'The monks had a lease of all the lands hereabouts at the time, and they were careful enough of them, too, I can tell you. But what should happen only that the MacCarthys got the notion to drive a road through the monastery lands, and that didn't go down well with the monks. Such wrangling and arguing you never heard in all your days. Anyway, the MacCarthys persisted, and the abbot cursed them, and a great plague fell on them. I needn't tell you they got mighty frightened — so frightened that they started to send gifts of oats and potatoes into the monastery, hoping to appease the abbot. But there was no lifting of the plague.

'In desperation they decided to send a deputation to the monks. And then it turned out that the gifts had never been delivered to the abbot! The O'Deas had got them and kept them for themselves. Such *ruaille buaille!* There was a huge enquiry. Donagh blamed his wife, and Mary blamed her husband, and the abbot was so disgusted with them and their lies that he banished them from the place altogether. Not only that but he put a

curse of sorts on them, to the effect that they would be separated as far apart from each other as the island of Ireland would permit. It wasn't a Christian or a Catholic thing for an abbot to do, but sure I suppose that kind of thing might have been all right in them days.

'Anyway, that's the way it came to pass. Mary wandered away down to the far south-west of County Cork, and her husband found himself away up in County Down, and as proof of what I tell you we have Muntervarry in Cork and they've Donaghadee in Down.

'Now,' he said, satisfaction in his voice. 'There's one for your book.'

He flicked the reins on the horse's back, and as he continued his journey towards the south the slow rattle of his cart echoed cheerily across the valley of the River Bride.

T. CROFTON CROKER

The Giant's Stairs

On the road between Passage and Cork is an old mansion called Ronayne's Court, and here it was that Maurice Ronayne and his wife Margaret Gould kept house. They were a well-to-do couple, and their only son was called Philip after no less a person than the King of Spain. He was a talented boy, and father and mother were justly proud of his accomplishments.

One morning Master Phil, then just seven years old, was missing. No one could tell what had become of him, and though servants were sent in all directions to search for him all returned without any tidings of him. A large reward was offered but it produced no information, and years rolled away without the parents having obtained any account of the fate of their lost child.

There lived at this time, near Carrigaline, one Robin Kelly, a blacksmith. He was what is termed a handy man, and his abilities were held in high esteem by the lads and lasses of the neighbourhood for, apart from shoeing horses and making plough-irons, he interpreted dreams for the young ladies, sang at their weddings, and was so good-natured a fellow at a christening that he was sponsor to half the country around.

Now it happened that Robin had a dream himself, and young Philip Ronayne appeared to him in it. Robin thought he saw the boy mounted on a beautiful white horse, and that he told him how he had been carried off and made a page to the Giant Mahon MacMahon who held his court in the hard heart of the rock overlooking the Harbour.

'The seven years of my service are clean out, Robin,' he told him, 'and if you release me this night I will be the making of you for ever after.'

'And how am I to know but this is all a dream?' Robin asked, cunning enough even in his sleep.

'Take that for a token,' said the boy, and at the words the white horse struck out with one of his hind legs and gave Robin such a kick in the forehead that, thinking he was a dead man, he roared and woke up yelling *mile murdar*. He was still in bed, but he had the mark of the blow, the regular print of a horse-shoe, on his forehead as red as blood.

Robin Kelly, who never before found himself puzzled at the dream of any other person, did not know what to think of his own. He knew Cork Harbour, and he was well acquainted with the Giant's Stairs — those great masses of rock piled one above the other which rise like a flight of steps from very deep water against the bold cliff of Carrigmahon. Nor are they badly suited for stairs to those whose legs are of sufficient length to stride over a moderate-sized house or to clear the space of a mile in a hop, step, and jump. Both of these feats the great MacMahon was said to have performed in the days of Finnian glory, and the common tradition of the country placed his dwelling within the cliff up whose side the stairs led.

Such was the impression which the dream made on Robin that he determined to put its truth to the test. It occurred to him, however, before setting out on his adventure, that a plough-iron might be no bad companion so, putting one on his shoulder, off he marched in the cool of the evening through the Hawk's Glen to Monkstown. Here lived an old friend of his, Tom Clancy by name, and on hearing Robin's dream he promised him the use of his skiff and offered to assist in rowing it to the Giant's Stairs.

It was a beautiful still night, and the little boat glided swiftly along. The regular dip of the oars, the distant song of a sailor, and sometimes the voice of a belated traveller at the ferry of Carrigaloe, alone broke the quietness. The tide was in their favour, and in a few minutes Robin and his friend rested on their oars under the dark shadow of the Giant's Stairs.

Robin looked anxiously for the entrance to the giant's palace which, it was said, could be found by anyone seeking it at midnight. But his impatience had hurried him there before time and, after waiting a considerable space in a state of suspense, Robin, with pure vexation, could not help exclaiming to his companion, 'Tis a pair of fools we are, Tom Clancy, for coming here at all on the strength of a dream.'

Just as he spoke they saw a faint light glimmering from the cliff, and it increased gradually until a porch big enough for a king's palace unfolded itself almost on a level with the water. They pulled the skiff directly towards the opening, and Robin Kelly, seizing his plough-iron, boldly entered with a strong hand and a stout heart.

Wild and strange was that entrance. It appeared to be formed of grim and grotesque faces, blending so strangely each with the other that it was impossible to define any. The chin of one formed the nose of another. What appeared to be a fixed and stern eye, if dwelt upon, changed to a gaping mouth. The lines of a lofty forehead grew into a majestic and flowing beard. The more Robin allowed himself to contemplate the forms around him the more terrific they became, and the stony expression of this crowd of faces assumed a savage ferocity as his imagination converted feature after feature into a different shape and character. Leaving the twilight in which these forms were visible he advanced through a dark and devious passage, whilst a deep and rumbling noise sounded as if the rock was about to close upon him and swallow him up alive for ever. Now, indeed, Robin felt afraid.

'Robin, Robin,' he said, 'if you were a fool for coming here, what in the name of fortune are you now?'

But, as before, he had scarcely spoken when he saw a small light twinkling through the darkness like a star in the midnight sky. He proceeded towards the light, and came at last into a spacious chamber from the roof of which hung the solitary lamp that had guided him. Several gigantic figures were seated around a massive stone table, as if in serious deliberation, but no word disturbed the breathless silence which prevailed. Mahon MacMahon himself sat at the head of this table.

He was the first to perceive Robin and, instantly starting up, demanded in a voice of thunder, 'WHAT SEEK YOU?'

'I come,' answered Robin with as much boldness as he could put on, for his heart was almost fainting within him, 'I come to claim Philip Ronayne whose time of service is out this night.'

'And who sent you here?' said the giant.

''Twas of my own accord I came,' said Robin.

'Then you must single him out from among my pages,' said the giant, 'And if you fix on the wrong one your life is forfeit. Follow me!'

He led Robin into a lighted hall of vast extent along either side of which were rows of beautiful children, all apparently seven years old, dressed in green and every one exactly dressed alike.

'Now,' said Mahon, 'you are free to take Philip Ronayne if you will, but remember — I give but one choice.'

Robin was sadly perplexed. There were hundreds upon hundreds of children, and he had no very clear recollection of the boy he sought. But he walked along the hall, by the side of Mahon, as if nothing was the matter, although the great giant's iron dress clanked fearfully at every step, sounding louder than Robin's own sledge battering on his anvil.

They had nearly reached the end without speaking when Robin, seeing that the only means he had was to make friends with the giant, determined to try what effect a few words might have.

' 'Tis a fine wholesome appearance the poor children carry,' he remarked, 'although they have been here so long shut out from the fresh air and sunshine. 'Tis tenderly your honour must have reared them!'

'Ay,' said the giant, 'that is true for you. Give me your hand, for you are, I believe, a very honest fellow for a blacksmith.'

Robin, at the first look, did not much like the huge size of the hand, and therefore presented his plough-iron which the giant seized and twisted in his grasp round and round again as if it had been a potato stalk. On seeing this all the children set up a shout of laughter. In the midst of their mirth Robin thought he heard his name called and, cocking ear and eye, he put his hand on the boy whom he fancied to have spoken.

'Let me live or die for it, but this is young Phil Ronayne,' he cried.

'It is Philip Ronayne — happy Philip Ronayne,' the children shouted in return, and in an instant the hall became dark. Crashing noises added to the confusion, but Robin held fast to his prize and found himself lying, in the grey dawn of the morning, at the head of the Giant's Stairs with the boy clasped in his arms.

The story of Robin's wonderful adventure soon spread through the country. Passage, Monkstown, Carrigaline — the whole barony of Kerricurrihy — rang with it. He received ample reward from the grateful parents at Ronayne's Court, and Philip himself lived to be an old man, remarkable to the day of his death for his skill in working brass and iron, which he had learned during his seven years' apprenticeship to the Giant Mahon MacMahon.

T. CROFTON CROKER

Hanlon's Mill

One autumn evening Michael Noonan went over to Jack Brien, the shoemaker at Ballyduff, to collect the pair of brogues which Jack was mending for him. It was a pretty walk along by the riverside and down by the oak-wood, but very lonesome.

By the time he got to Hanlon's Mill it was fairly between lights; the day was clean gone and the moon was not yet up. Melancholy enough looked the walls of that same mill, gone to ruin many a long year, with the great old wheel black with age, all covered over with moss and ferns, with the bushes all hanging down about it. There it stood, silent and motionless, and a sad contrast it was to its former busy clack, with the stream that once gave it power rippling idly by.

Old Hanlon was a man who had great knowledge of all sorts. There was not a herb that grew in the field but he could tell the name of it and its use. Indeed he had written a big book on the subject — every word of it in Irish. He kept a school once, and could teach Latin, and I hear tell as how the great Burke went to school to him. Master Edmund lived up at the old house, which was then in the family; the Nagles got it afterwards but they sold it.

Suddenly, as Michael Noonan was walking smartly across the Inch, he heard, coming down out of the wood, such blowing of horns and hallooing, and the cry of all the hounds in the world, and the galloping of the horses, and the voice of the whipper-in and he shouting out, and the echo over from the grey rock across the river giving back every word as plainly as it was spoken.

At first he thought it must be Mr. Wrixon and his hounds, then he realised it was too late in the day for them; he also recollected that the Duhallows were out in quite another quarter that day. He paused, but nothing could he see. Then he was certain that he heard the clack of old Hanlon's Mill going through all the noise — and he knew that nothing good could come out of the noise there.

You can be sure he ran as fast as fear and his legs could carry him and never once looked behind him. But the shouting and hallooing followed him every step of the way till he got to Jack Brien's door.

Well, Michael Noonan got his brogues, and well heeled they were, and well pleased was he. He was just about recovering from his fright when who should come in to Jack Brien's but a gossip of his, one Darby Haynes, a mighty decent man, who had a horse and a car of his own and who used to be travelling with it, taking loads like the royal mail coach between Cork and Limerick. Darby, when he was at home, was a near neighbour of Michael Noonan.

'Is it home you're going with the brogues this blessed night?' said Darby to him.

'Where else would it be?' replied Mick. 'But by my word, it's not across the Inch I'll be going, after all I heard coming here. 'Tis to no good that old Hanlon's Mill is busy again.'

'True for you,' said Darby. 'Then, as you'll be going home by the road, maybe you'd take the horse and car home for me, by way of company. I'm waiting here to see the son of a sister of mine that I expect from Kilcolman.'

'That same I'll do,' answered Mick, 'with a thousand welcomes.'

Mick drove the car fair and easy. He was always tender-hearted and good to animals, and he knew that the poor beast had had a long journey. The night was calm and beautiful. The moon was better than a quarter old, and was shining down sweetly upon the gentle Awbeg. Soon Mick left the open road and came to a part where the trees grew on both sides. He proceeded for some time in the half and half light of the moon. Sometimes it was so dark that he could hardly see the horse's head, then the moonbeams would stream through the open boughs and dapple the road with light and shade.

Mick got clear of the plantation with a sense of relief and fell to watching the bright crescent of a moon in the little pools at the roadside. Suddenly it disappeared, as if a great cloud had come over it. He looked up at the sky. The moon was still shining brightly, but he was astonished to find, close alongside the car, a great high black coach drawn by six black horses with long black tails reaching almost down to the ground, and a coachman dressed all in black sitting upon the box. But what surprised Mick more than anything was that he could see no sign of a head either upon the coachman or horses. The coach swept rapidly by him, and he could see the horses' hooves pounding the ground as if they were in a fine fast gallop, the coachman touching them up with his long whip, and the wheels spinning round like hoddy-doddies. But he could hear absolutely nothing, only the regular step of Darby's horse and the squeaking of the gudgeons of the car which were in want of a little grease.

Poor Mick's heart almost died within him, and he watched in terror as the black coach swept away and was soon lost amongst the distant trees. He saw nothing more of it, nor indeed did he notice anything else for the rest of his journey. He got home just as the moon was going down behind Mount Hillery, took the tackle off the horse, turned him out into the field and got to his bed.

Next morning, early, he was standing at the roadside thinking of all that had happened the night before. Then he saw Dan Madden, Mr. Wrixon's huntsman, coming down the hill on the master's best horse, as hard as ever he went at the tail of the hounds. Mick's mind instantly sprang to the conclusion that all was not right, so he ran out in the middle of the road and caught hold of Dan's bridle when he came up.

'Mick, dear, for the love of God, don't stop me now,' cried Dan.

'Why, what's the hurry?' asked Mick.

'Why, the master! He's off, he's off — he'll never cross a horse again till the day of judgment!'

'Why, what would ail his honour?' said Mick. 'Sure it is no later than yesterday morning that I was talking to him and he stout and hearty.'

'Stout and hearty was he,' answered Madden. 'And was he not out with me in the kennels last night when I was feeding the dogs? And didn't he come out to the stable and give a ball to Peg Pullaway with his own hand, and he told me he'd ride Old General today. Who'd have thought that the first thing I'd see this morning would be the mistress standing at my bedside, and bidding me get up and ride off like fire for Doctor Johnson, for the master had got a fit?'

Poor Dan's grief choked his voice. 'Oh, Mick, if you have a heart in you, run over yourself for Kate Finnegan, the midwife. She's a cruel skilful woman, and maybe she might save the master till I get the doctor.'

Dan struck his spurs into the hunter, and Michael Noonan flung off his newly mended brogues, and cut across the fields to Kate Finnegan's.

But neither the doctor nor Katy were of any avail, and the next night's moon saw Ballygibblin a house of morning.

JAMES LYONS

Outlaw of the Gearagh

The north road from Cork city to Macroom lies along
the river valley of the Lee. For nine miles the road twists
and slides with the river, caressing every gentle contour
of the hillside slopes, looking down on the green pastures
in the valley and on the small woodlands that cluster
here and there. For a few miles it explores the little valley
of the Dripsey, but eventually returns to the Lee and
keeps it company to within a mile of Macroom. There
it crosses the Sullane, a river in appearance and size
comparable with the Lee at this point. It falters for a
moment, undecided, as though tempted to follow the
Sullane upriver to look at Macroom but, joining the
southern road from Cork, it forms a tee-junction and
leaves the choice of ways to the traveller.

If you turn right and pass through Macroom you will
have Ballyvourney, Killarney, and the whole of Kerry
on your horizon. But for the purpose of this story, follow
the road left, retracing your steps a little way towards
the city. The next turn right will set your course for
the mountain districts of West Cork. For twenty miles
that road retains its link with the Lee, but follow it for
less than four miles. The hills slope towards the south,
gently but unevenly, and the road winding along their
sides is turbulent at times. Sometimes it swoops viciously
on double corners, sometimes it climbs steeply over long-
flung buttresses of rock. And on its way it skirts the
edges of vast fastnesses, wild, romantic and, in their own
remote way, picturesque. This is the Gearagh.

Once upon a time there was a great lake there, but

57

over the centuries the lakelands silted up and the area became a vast marsh, hiding beneath the stunted trees and tangled bushes that inevitably sprawl over wet lands everywhere. The Gearagh, as it was known, was veined with varied and vagrant waterways and at one time formed an impassible barrier between the districts lying north and south of it. Today the Gearagh, like many another unique feature of the countryside beside the Lee, has faded from the landscape. The artificial floods rising behind the dams of Inniscarra and Carrigadrohid have spread their waters over the entire area and it has become a lake once more.

In the early years of the eighteenth century a carpenter, John Murphy, lived at Tarelton on the southern side of the Gearagh. He was a tough, lean, enduring man of middle years with red hair, who was known over a wide area as Séan Ruadh. He had been abroad with the Irish Brigade but had returned home some time before 1725, married, and settled down in his native place. At the time the Rapparees were conducting their campaign to prevent the administration of the Penal Laws. Séan, who had retained one of his foreign-service guns in spite of the strict prohibition on arms, had become a prominent member. He was an excellent shot and was hated by the landed gentry, not only because he was a Rapparee but also for his poaching.

Over at Macroom, in the castle which was once the property of MacCarthy More of Muskerry, lived a Mr. Hedges, an English settler who had purchased the castle about the year 1704, and with it a considerable acreage of land. He was just and honourable, frowned on persecution in all its forms, wielded great influence, and maintained order with a stern hand. His disapproval of the sometimes brutal activities of the Rapparees was no secret, and it led to a misunderstanding which turned Seán Ruadh into a hunted outlaw.

The Rapparees had staged an attack somewhere

between Bandon and Macroom, and Seán Ruadh, who
had been away from his farm working as journeyman
carpenter among farmers and gentry throughout the
countryside, was thought to have taken a leading part.
Garrison soldiers from Bandon were active in the search
for suspects, and one night when Seán was back home
his holding was surrounded. But his dog gave the alarm,
and he succeeded in escaping by draping his shirt on
an old cart-wheel, which he sent rolling down the hill
to draw off the soldiers.

Seán believed that Hedges had some part in his
attempted capture. He called on a cousin some way
distant who was a tenant of Hedges and, as custom
demanded, was rearing two promising pups from his
landlord's hunting pack. Seán killed the pups, an act
which provoked Hedges, who had had nothing to do
with the soldiers' raid, into declaring that he would bring
him to justice.

Seán took refuge in the Gearagh, uncharted and comparatively unknown at the time, and when provisions ran out he sent his dog, with a basket tied to its neck, into Macroom where friends filled it with food and drink. Any curious follower who sought the secret of the outlaw's hide-out was led by the dog-through bog and bush into places from which it was not easy to return.

One evening Seán came out of the Gearagh and entered the castle demesne at Macroom. Hedges sat near a window talking to his friend and associate, Mr. White of Bantry. A candle in its holder stood on the table between them, and, stepping from his hiding-place Seán fired, shooting the candle out of its holder.

Hedges acknowledged that shot as an act of intimidation and, accepting the challenge, commissioned a company of soldiers to come from Cork to bring the outlaw to justice. News of this new development reached Seán through secret channels, and before the soldiers had arrived he had disappeared to shelter in a friend's house on the southern shores of the Inchigeela lakes.

In the meantime the soldiers from Cork were combing the Gearagh for their elusive quarry, without success. After one unsuccessful expedition the officer of the company was boasting to Hedges about the marksmanship of his sergeant, claiming that no one in the Macroom area could hope to outshoot him. Hedges recollected Seán Ruadh and the candle shot and, although he had no idea where the outlaw was hiding out at the time, he suggested a contest between the two, pledging his protection to the outlaw and promising that no attempt would be made to take him. News of the challenge reached Seán through his friends, and he placed so much faith in Hedges's pledge that he came at the appointed time on the appointed day.

Great crowds from the surrounding countryside had come into Macroom to be present at the contest. Mr. White of Bantry had been appointed judge, and the competition was a simple one. A crown was set up on a board on the eastern wall of the castle yard, and the contestant who scored most hits from fifty paces was to be acknowledged victor.

Several shots were fired, and after this first stage the marksmen were declared equal. To decide the issue, a special target was then set up and, as had been arranged, it was Seán Ruadh's privilege to decide what that target would be. His choice was an exacting one. A knife was fixed to the board, edge to the contestants, and he who could hit the edge, slicing the bullet into two halves, would be the winner.

The sergeant missed. The assembled people stirred, whispered, and drew close together. Seán moved into position, took aim, and fired. A sharp crack sounded on the board but the knife remained in position. Several hundred expectant eyes followed Mr. White as he approached the target. He found embedded in the timber, at each side of the knife's blade, half of a bullet.

Seán had won, but when the crowd turned to applaud his achievement their hero had flown. Tradition has it that he lived thereafter free from molestation to an exceptional old age. He tilled his small holding and worked at his trade, journeying as of old back and forth among the people. Wherever he went he was well received and respected, and when the end came it was in the peace and comfort of his own home.

T. CROFTON CROKER

Daniel O'Rourke

Daniel O'Rourke lived at the bottom of Hungry Hill, at the right-hand side of the road that runs along the shores of Bantry Bay from Castletownbere to Glengarriff. One sunny afternoon in the summer of 1813, when he was then an old man, he sat smoking his pipe under an ancient poplar tree, recalling the adventures that befell him on the night he slept under the walls of the Pooka's Tower.

'I am often asked to tell the story,' he began, 'so that this is not the first time. The master's son had come home from foreign parts, and a dinner was given in the grounds to all the neighbours. Well, we had everything of the best, and plenty of it, and we ate and we drank and we danced, and it happened that in the course of the evening I got, as a body might say, tipsy, for I can't remember ever at all how I left the place. Only leave it I did and that's certain, for as I was crossing the stepping-stones of the ford of Ballyashenogh I missed my foot, and souse I fell into the water.

'Death alive!' thought I, 'I'll be drowned now!' so I began swimming, swimming, swimming away for dear life, till at last I got ashore on a desolate island.

'I wandered and wandered about there, without knowing where I was going, until at last I got into a big bog. The moon was shining as bright as day, and I looked east and west, and north and south and every way, and nothing did I see but bog, bog, bog. I couldn't think how I got into it, and my heart grew cold with fear, so sure and certain I was that it would be my burying

Bantry Bay

place. I sat down upon a stone which, as good luck would have it, was close by me, and began to scratch my head and sing the *Ullagone,* when all of a sudden the moon grew black, and I looked up, and saw an eagle — as fine a one as ever flew from the Kingdom of Kerry. He looked me in the face and says to me, "Daniel O'Rourke," says he, "how do you do?"

"Very well, I thank you," says I, wondering out of my senses all the time how an eagle came to speak like a Christian.

"What brings you here, Dan?" says he.

"Nothing at all," says I, "only I wish I was safe home again."

"Is it out of the island you want to go, Dan?" says he.

" 'Tis," says I, and I up and told him that as I didn't know how I got into the bog I didn't know how to get out of it.

"Dan," says he, after a minute's thought, "as you are a decent sober man who never flings stones at me or mine, nor cries out after us in the fields — my life for yours! So get up on my back, and grip me well for fear you'd fall off, and I'll fly you out of the bog."

'Well, I had no choice so, thinks I to myself, faint heart never won fair lady and this is fair persuadance. "I thank you," says I, "and I'll take your kind offer."

'I therefore mounted upon the back of the eagle, holding him tight enough by the throat, and up he flew in the air like a lark. Up, up, up — God knows how far up he flew. Little I knew the trick he was about to serve me!

"Why then," says I to him very civilly, thinking he did not know the right road home, "if you'd fly down a bit, you're now just over my house, and you could put me down there, and many thanks."

"Arrah, Dan," says he, "do you think me a fool? Look down in the next field, and don't you see two men and a gun? By my word it would be no joke to be shot this way to oblige a drunken blackguard that I picked up off a cold stone in a bog."

'Well, sir, he kept flying up and up, and I asking him every minute to fly down, and at last where should we come to but to the moon itself. Now you can't see it from here but there is, or there was in my time, a reaping-hook sticking out of the side of it.

"Dan," says the eagle, "I'm tired with this long flight. I had no notion 'twas so far. So you must get off, and sit down on the moon until I rest myself. You can catch fast hold of the reaping-hook that's sticking out of the side of the moon, and 'twill keep you up."

"I won't then," says I.

"Maybe not," says he, "but if you don't, my man, I shall just give you a shake and one slap of my wing, and send you down to the ground where every bone in your body will be smashed as small as a drop of dew on a cabbage-leaf in the morning."

'So, giving him a hearty curse in Irish, for fear he'd know what I said, I got off his back with a heavy heart, took hold of the reaping-hook and sat down upon the moon. And a mighty cold seat it was, I can tell you that.

'When he had me fairly landed he turned about on me, and says he, "I think I've nicked you now. You robbed my nest last year and, in return, you are freely welcome to cool your heels dangling upon the moon like a cockthrow." So saying, he spread out his great big wings, burst out laughing, and flew away like lightning.

'I bawled after him to stop, but I might have called and bawled for ever without his minding me, and I never saw him from that day to this. You may be sure I was in a disconsolate condition, and kept roaring out for the bare grief, when all at once a door opened right in the middle of the moon, creaking on its hinges as if it had not been opened for a month, and out there walks — who do you think — but the man in the moon himself? I knew him by his bush.

"Good morrow to you, Daniel O'Rourke," says he. "How do you do, and what brought you here?" So I told him how the thief of an eagle promised to fly me out of the bog, and how instead of that he had flown me up to the moon.

"Dan," says the man in the moon, taking a pinch of snuff, "you must not stay here."

"Indeed, sir," says I, " 'tis much against my will I'm here at all, but how am I to get back?"

"That's your business, Dan," says he. "Mine is to tell you that here you must not stay — so be off in less than no time."

"I'm doing no harm," says I. "Only holding on hard by the reaping-hook lest I fall off."

"That's what you must not do, Dan," says he.

"Pray, sir," says I, "may I ask how many you are in family, that you would not give a poor traveller lodging. I'm sure 'tis not so often you're troubled with strangers coming to see you, for 'tis a long way."

"I'm by myself, Dan," says he, "but you'd better let go the reaping-hook."

"Faith, and with your leave," says I, "I'll not let go the grip, and the more you bid me the more I won't let go."

"We'll see how that is to be," says he, and back he went, giving the door such a great bang after him, for it was plain he was huffed, that I thought the moon and all would fall down with it.

'Well, I was preparing myself to try strength with him when back again he came with the kitchen cleaver in his hand and, without saying a word, he gave two bangs to the handle of the reaping-hook that was keeping me up, and whap! — it came in two.

"Good morning to you, Dan," says the spiteful little old blackguard when he saw me falling down with a bit of the handle in my hand. "I thank you for your visit, and fair weather after you, Daniel."

'I had not time to make any answer to him, for I was tumbling over and over, and rolling and rolling, at the rate of a fox-hunt.

"God help me," says I, "but this is a pretty pickle for a decent man to be seen in at this time of night."

'The word was not out of my mouth when whiz! — what should fly by close to my ear but a flock of wild geese, all the way from my own bog of Ballyasheenogh, else how should they know *me?* The old gander, who was their general, turned about his head and cried out to me, "Is that you, Dan?"

"The same," says I, not a bit daunted now at what he said, for I was by this time used to all kinds of bedevilment. And besides, I knew him of old.

"Good morrow to you," says he. "I think 'tis falling you are, Daniel."

"You may say that," says I.

"And where are you going all the way so fast?" asks the gander.

'So I told him how I had taken the drop, and how I came on the island, and how I lost my way in the bog, and how the thief of an eagle flew me up to the moon, and how the man in the moon turned me out.

"Dan," says he, "I'll save you. Put out your hand and catch me by the leg, and I'll fly you home."

"Sweet is your hand in a pitcher of honey, my jewel," says I. So I caught the gander by the leg, and away I and the other geese flew after him as fast as hops.

'We flew, and we flew, and we flew, until we came over the wide ocean. I knew it well, for I saw Cape Clear to my right hand, sticking up out of the water.

"Ah, my lord," says I to the goose, for I thought it best to keep a civil tongue in my head anyway. "Fly to land, if you please."

"That's impossible for a while, Dan," says he, "because we're going to Arabia."

"To Arabia?" says I. "That's surely some place in foreign parts far away. Oh, Mr. Goose, why then to

67

be sure I'm a man to be pitied among you."

'Just as we were talking a ship hove in sight, scudding so beautifully before the wind.

"Ah, then," says I, "will you drop me on the ship, if you please?"

"We are not fair over it," says he.

"We are," says I.

"We are not," says he. "If I dropped you now you would go splash into the sea."

"I would not," says I. "I know better than that, for it is just clean under us, so let me drop now, at once."

"If you must, you must," says he. "There, take your own way," and he opened his claw, and faith he was right! Sure enough I came down plump into the very bottom of the salt sea. Down to the very bottom I went, and I gave myself up then for ever. A whale walked up to me, scratching himself after his night's sleep, and looked me full in the face, and never the word did he say but lifting up his tail he splashed me all over again with the cold salt water till there wasn't a dry stitch upon my whole carcass.

'And then I heard somebody saying — 'twas a voice I knew, too, "Get up, you drunken brute, off o' that!" and with that I woke up, and there was Judy with a tub full of water which she was splashing all over me. For, rest her soul, though she was a good wife she never could bear to see me in drink, and had a bitter hand of her own.

"Get up," she said again, "and of all the places in the parish would no place serve your turn to lie down upon but under the old walls of Carrigaphouca? An uneasy resting I am sure you had of it."

'And sure enough I had, for I was fairly bothered out of my senses with eagles and men in the moon and flying ganders and whales, driving me through bogs and up to the moon and down to the bottom of the green ocean. If I was in drink ten times over, long would it be before I'd lie down in the same spot again.'

T. CROFTON CROKER

The Haunted Cellar

There are few people who have not heard of the MacCarthys, one of the real old Irish families with the true Milesian blood running in their veins as thick as buttermilk. Many were the clans of this family in the south of Ireland, and all of them were noted for their hospitality to strangers. But not one of the name, or of any other, exceeded Justin MacCarthy of Ballina-carthy at putting plenty to eat and drink upon his table, and there was a right hearty welcome for everyone who should share it with him. Many a wine-cellar would be ashamed of the name if that at Ballinacarthy was the proper pattern for one. Large as that cellar was, it was so crowded with bins of wine, and long rows of pipes and hogsheads and casks, that it would take more time to count them than any sober man could spare in such a place, especially with plenty to drink about him and a hearty welcome to do so.

There are many who will think that the butler in such a house would have little to complain of, and the whole country around would have agreed with them — if a man could have been found to remain as Mr. MacCar-thy's butler for any length of time worth speaking of. Yet no one who had been in his service gave him a bad word.

'We have no fault to find with the master,' they would say, 'and if he could but get any one to fetch his wine from the cellar we might, every one of us, have grown grey in the house, and lived quiet and contented enough in his service until the end of our days.'

' 'Tis a queer thing that, surely,' thought young Jack Leary, a lad who had been brought up from a mere child in the stables of Ballinacarthy to assist in taking care of the horses, and had occasionally lent a hand in the butler's pantry. ' 'Tis a mighty queer thing, surely, that one man after another cannot content himself with the best place in the house of a good master, but that every one of them must quit, all through the means, as they say, of the wine-cellar. If the master would but make me his butler I warrant never the word more would be heard of grumbling at his bidding to go to the wine-cellar.'

Young Leary accordingly watched for a favourable opportunity of presenting himself to the notice of his master.

A few mornings after, Mr. MacCarthy went into his stable-yard rather earlier than usual, and called loudly for the groom to saddle his horse as he intended going out with the hounds. But there was no groom to answer, and young Jack Leary led Rainbow out of the stable.

'Where is William?' inquired Mr. MacCarthy.

'Sir?' said Jack, and Mr. MacCarthy repeated the question.

'Is it William, please your honour?' returned Jack. 'Why, then, to tell the truth, he had just one drop too much last night.'

'Where did he get it?' said Mr. MacCarthy. 'For, since Thomas went away, the key of the wine-cellar has been in my pocket, and I have been obliged to fetch what was drunk myself.'

'Sorrow a know I know,' said Leary, 'unless the cook might have given him the least taste of whiskey. But,' he continued, 'may I make so bold as just to ask your honour one question?'

'Speak out, Jack,' said Mr. MacCarthy.

'Why, then ... does your honour want a butler?'

'Can you recommend me one?' returned his master, with a smile of good humour upon his countenance. 'One who will not be afraid of going to my wine-cellar!'

'Is the wine-cellar all the matter?' said young Leary.

'Devil a doubt I have of myself then for that.'

'So you mean to offer me your services in the capacity of butler?' said Mr. MacCarthy with some surprise.

'Exactly so,' answered Leary, now for the first time looking up from the ground.

'Well, I believe you to be a good lad, and have no objection to giving you a trial.'

'Long may your honour reign over us, and the Lord spare you to us!' ejaculated Leary as his master rode off, and he continued for some time to gaze after him with a vacant stare which slowly and gradually assumed a look of importance.

'Jack Leary,' said he, at length. 'Jack — is it Jack?' in a tone of wonder. 'Faith, 'tis not Jack now, but Mr. John, the butler!'

And with an air of becoming consequence he strode out of the stable-yard towards the kitchen.

When Mr. MacCarthy returned from hunting he sent for Jack Leary, as he still continued to call his new butler.

'Jack,' said he, 'I believe you are a trustworthy lad, and here are the keys of my cellar. I have asked the gentlemen with whom I hunted today to dine with me, and I hope they may be satisfied at the way in which you will wait on them at table. Above all, let there be no want of wine after dinner.'

Mr. John, having a tolerably quick eye for such things and being naturally a handy lad, spread his cloth accordingly, laid his plates and knives and forks in the same manner he had seen his predecessors in office perform these mysteries, and really, though it was his first time, he got through attendance at dinner very well.

It was waxing near midnight when Mr. MacCarthy rang the bell three times. This was a signal for more wine. Jack proceeded to the cellar to get a fresh supply but not, it must be confessed, without some little hesitation. Mr. MacCarthy's grandfather had built the mansion of Ballinacarthy upon the site of an old castle which had belonged to his ancestors, and in the construction of his magnificent wine-cellar had availed himself of a deep vault which had been excavated out of the solid rock in former times as a place of retreat and security. The descent to this vault was by a flight of steep stone stairs, and here and there in the wall were narrow passages and certain projections which cast deep shadows and looked very frightful when any one went down there with a flickering light. Jack carried a lantern and the key of the cellar in his right hand, and in his left a basket which he considered large enough to contain enough wine for the remainder of the evening.

He arrived at the door without any trouble but when he put the key in the lock he thought he heard a strange kind of laughing within the cellar. At the same time some empty bottles that stood upon the floor outside vibrated so violently that they struck against each other.

Leary paused for a moment, and looked about him with caution. He then boldly seized the handle of the key, and turned it in the lock with all his strength, as if he doubted his own power of doing so. The door flew open with a most tremendous crash.

To recount what the poor fellow saw then would be impossible, for he seems not to have been very clear himself. What he told the cook next morning was that he heard a roaring and bellowing like a mad bull, and that all the pipes and hogsheads and casks in the cellar went rocking backwards and forwards with so much force that he thought every one of them would have been staved in, and that he himself would have been drowned or smothered in wine.

Certain it is, however, that when he recovered from the shock he made his way back as well as he could to the dining-room, where he found his master and the company very impatient for his return.

'What kept you?' said Mr. MacCarthy in an angry voice. 'Where's the wine I rang for half an hour ago.'

'The wine is in the cellar, I hope, sir,' said Jack, trembling violently. 'I hope 'tis not all lost!'

'What do you mean, fool?' exclaimed Mr. MacCarthy in a still more angry tone. 'Why did you not bring some with you?' Jack looked wildly about him, and only uttered a deep groan.

'Gentlemen,' said Mr. MacCarthy to his guests, 'this is too much. When I next see you to dinner I hope it will be in another house, for it is impossible I can remain longer in one where a man has no command over his own wine-cellar, and cannot get a butler to do his duty. I have long thought of moving from Ballinacarthy, and I am now determined, with the blessing of God, to leave it tomorrow. But wine you shall have tonight.'

So saying, he rose from the table, took the key and lantern from his half-stupefied servant and descended the narrow stairs which led to his cellar.

When he arrived at the door, which he found open, he thought he heard a noise as if of rats or mice scrambling over the casks, and on advancing perceived a little figure about six inches in height seated astride a pipe of the oldest port in the place and bearing a spigot upon his shoulder. Raising the lantern Mr. MacCarthy contemplated the little fellow with wonder. He wore a red night-cap on his head; a short leather apron which, from his attitude, fell on one side; stockings of a light blue colour, so long as nearly to cover the entire of his leg; and shoes with huge silver buckles and high heels. His face was like a withered winter apple and his nose, which was of a bright crimson colour, wore a delicate purple bloom like that of a plum about the tip. Yet his eyes twinkled, and his mouth twitched up at one side with an arch grin.

'Ha, scoundrel,' exclaimed Mr. MacCarthy, 'have I found you at last, disturber of my cellar? What are you doing there?'

'Sure, and master,' returned the little fellow, looking up at him with one eye and with the other throwing a sly glance towards the spigot on his shoulder, 'aren't we going to move tomorrow? And sure you would not leave your own little *cluricaune* Naggeneen behind you?'

'Oh,' thought Mr. MacCarthy, 'if you are to follow me, Master Naggeneen, I don't see much use in quitting Ballinacarthy!'

So, filling with wine the basket which young Leary in his fright had left behind him, and locking the cellar door, he rejoined his guests.

For some years after Mr. MacCarthy had always to fetch the wine for his table himself, as the little *cluricaune* Naggeneen seemed to feel a personal respect towards him. He lived in his paternal mansion to a good round age, and was famous to the last for the excellence of his wine and the conviviality of his company. But at the time of his death that same conviviality had nearly emptied his wine-cellar, and as it was never so well filled again, nor so often visited, the revels of Master Naggeneen became less celebrated and are now only spoken of among the legendary lore of the country. It is even said that the poor little fellow took the declension of the cellar so to heart that he became negligent and careless of himself, and that he has been sometimes seen going about with hardly a *scríd* to cover him.

T. CROFTON CROKER

The Spirit Horse

When he had just turned fourteen years, Morty Sullivan ran away from his father and mother, and many and many a tear they shed on his account. It is said they both died heart-broken for his loss, for all they ever learned about him was that he went on board of a ship bound for America.

Thirty years after they had been laid peacefully in their graves there came a stranger to Berehaven inquiring after them. It was their son Morty and, to speak the truth of him, his heart did seem full of sorrow when he heard that his parents were dead and gone. As an atonement for his sin he was recommended to perform a pilgrimage to the chapel of St. Gobnait at Ballyvourney.

This he readily undertook, and anxious to lose no time commenced his journey the same afternoon. He had not proceeded many miles before evening came on. There was no moon, and the starlight was obscured by thick fog which ascended from the valleys. His way was through mountainous country with many cross-paths and by-ways, so that for a stranger like Morty, travelling without a guide, progress was slow. Anxious to reach his destination, however, he persevered.

The fog grew thicker and thicker, and at last he began to wonder if the track he was following led to St. Gobnait's chapel or whether he had missed his way. Then, thankfully, he saw a light which he imagined not to be far off and he set out towards it. However, just as he thought he should be close to it, it suddenly receded and he could see it, a long way away, twinkling through the fog. Thus did he travel for many a weary mile, the light alternately just within reach, then vanishing into the far distance.

At length he came so close as to see that the light came from a fire, seated beside which he plainly saw an old woman. Then, indeed, did he doubt his own eyes! Much did he wonder that both the fire and the old woman should travel before him so many miles, and over such uneven roads. 'How can that burning fire move on so fast before me, and how can that old woman be sitting beside the moving fire?' he wondered.

These words had no sooner passed through his thoughts than he found himself, without taking another step, beside this extraordinary fire, before which the old woman was sitting munching her supper. With every wag of her jaw her eyes would roll fiercely upon Morty, as if she was angry at being disturbed, and he saw with more astonishment than ever that her eyes were neither black nor blue nor grey nor hazel, like human eyes, but of a wild red colour like the eyes of a ferret. If, previously he had wondered at the fire, much greater was his wonder at the old woman's appearance, and, stout-hearted as he was, he could not but look upon her with fear, judging that it was for no good purpose she supped in so

unfrequented a place at so late an hour, for it was near midnight. She said not one word, but munched and munched away while Morty looked at her in silence.

'What's your name?' at last demanded the old hag, a sulphureous puff coming from her mouth, her nostrils distending, and her eyes growing redder than ever.

Plucking up all his courage he replied, 'Morty Sullivan at your service,' meaning the latter words only in civility.

'Ubbubbo!' said the old woman. 'We'll soon see that,' and the red fire of her eyes turned into a pale green colour. Bold and fearless as Morty was, he trembled at hearing this dreadful exclamation.

'Take hold of my hand, Morty; I'll give you a horse to ride that will soon carry you to your journey's end.'

So saying, she led the way, the fire going before them, shooting out bright tongues of flame and flickering fiercely. Presently they came to a natural cavern in the side of the mountain, and the old hag called aloud, in a most discordant voice, for her horse. In a moment a jet-black steed started from its gloomy stable, the rock floor ringing with a sepulchral echo to the clanging hoofs.

'Mount, Morty, mount,' cried she, seizing him with supernatural strength and forcing him upon the back of the horse. Morty, finding human power of no avail, muttered, 'Oh that I had spurs!' and tried to grasp the horse's mane. But he only caught at a shadow which nevertheless bore him up and bounded forward with him, now springing down a fearful precipice, now clearing the rugged bed of a torrent and rushing like a dark midnight storm through the mountains.

The following morning, some pilgrims who came that way after making their rounds at Gougane Barra, discovered Morty Sullivan lying on the flat of his back under the steep cliff down which he had been flung by the Pooka. He was severely bruised by the fall, and is said to have sworn on the spot never again to take a full quart bottle of whiskey with him on a pilgrimage.

JAMES LYONS

The Legend of Rathgobáin

A long swathe of fertile hillside slopes away northward out of the valley of the Lee estuary, and levels off among the airy acres of *Cnocán na Biolaraighe;* no hillock merely, but an obstinate, energy-sapping, heart-testing, ranging plateau. This great watershed, dividing Lee from Blackwater, looks to north and south over half the ancient kingdom of Cork and commands a prospect of lavender-tinted mountains and haze-grey highlands on both horizons. The plateau itself is cleft and creviced into quirky glens, and venturesome *bohereens* wend through deciduous parklands and conifer forests. One of these runs north-eastward and, like a mountain stream gambolling, glancing and plunging, planing, glissading, it eventually loses itself in a secret-seeming valley of little rounded hills and furzy hollows. There, on a lump of rock, vaguely surrounded by a broken moat, stands the remnant of an old stone gable, and this according to local tradition was, and is still, called the Gobán Saor's Castle. The place, significantly enough, retains its name in Irish — *Rath Gobáin.*

Gobán Saor of the fabulous Tuatha de Danaan was an artisan of highest performance and skill, a great craftsman in stone, the man who, it is said, built the first Irish round tower. Whenever a bridge or a fort or a castle was to be constructed, his services were commissioned everywhere in the kingdom of Ireland, and far beyond it. He was an equally gifted metal-worker and swordmaker, and his reputation for nimble wit and wisdom made him the most respected of his contemporaries and the most talked-about in song and story.

Gobán Saor had one son and, as befitted the offspring of so accomplished a father, he too was a talented fellow, though his interests, as was natural to a vigorous, graceful, and energetic youth, were concentrated more on the sports at which he excelled. He was champion in the field but, endowed as he was with strength and agility, he was of considerable help to his father in the pursuit of his trade.

The old castle at Rath Gobáin was a hospitable house, and many's the lively hosting that found entertainment under its roof. The Gobán's wife was an able woman who conducted herself capably in the running of her home, and the whole household worked efficiently under her unerring direction. The Góban himself had no domestic problems while she lived, but when she died things began to run awry. Father and son had their various commissions to attend to, and the servants, though willing, lacked the initiative to work without the supervision of a mistress.

The Gobán had been turning those problems over in his mind, and one day he spoke to his son.

'A mhic, mo chroí,' he said to him, 'your mother is a sore loss to us. We cannot continue to keep house as it should be done under present conditions, and I can see only the one solution. I would not dream of putting another woman in your mother's place, but as you are of suitable age, and of no mean appearance, I think you ought to be casting an eye about for a capable girl to honour our establishment.'

Much the same notion had been in the son's mind for some time past, so he was not unwilling to turn an attentive ear to his father's suggestion.

'And how do you think I should go about it, father?' he asked.

'Tomorrow will be fair day in Lisgoold,' he was told. 'Be up at daybreak, and I will tell you what you must do. It's a sensible girl a man needs to run his affairs

79

for him. Go now, and get some sleep ... you have a tricky day ahead of you.'

So the son went away to bed; the Gobán himself went out and killed a sheep and skinned it.

Next morning before ever the sun peeped over the tops of the woods that stretched eastward from Rath Gobáin father and son came together in the great hall of the castle. The sheepskin was stretched to its full extent on the flagged floor, and both of them stood looking down on it.

'Now, my son, here is your mission. Take the skin to the fair, and do not sell it until you get the skin and the worth of it,' the Gobán advised, 'and who knows what luck may be yours?'

'Luck I'll be wanting, indeed,' the son thought to himself, but he said nothing and, lifting the skin on to the waiting donkey-cart, he trotted away towards Lisgoold.

Prospective buyers came, laughed a loud laugh, and went their way with many a cynical comment. A good-looking young man was one thing, but no girl wanted a part in that kind of foolish bargain. Somewhat abashed he prepared to return home at the end of the day, but just as he was about to leave the fair green a lissome keen-eyed slip of a girl chanced his way.

'Would you like to buy a fine sheepskin?' he asked her, not hopefully, but to his surprise she stood to examine it.

'What price do you want?' she asked him.

'I want the skin and the value of it,' he told her, diffidently enough she thought.

She looked at him for a long moment, merriment and calculation in her eyes, and he felt his heart turning a small somersault within him. That was the kind of girl she was.

'I'll take it,' she said simply. 'Come up to the house with me, and I'll seal the bargain.'

So up she hopped beside him on the little cart, the

skin on the boards behind them, and away they jogged on a by-road into the woods. She was an easy enough girl to get on with, with many a light-hearted quip and a laugh that sang like water spilling over the rim of a mountain spring. A mile or so along this *bohereen* they came to a cottage set back from the road, where two younger girls were busy about the garden.

'These are my sisters,' the girl explained, 'but come in till you meet my mother, and we'll pay your price.'

In they went into a neat kitchen-cum-living room and, although it was a warm evening, a turf fire glowed warmly in the open hearth. A plain deal dresser stood against the opposite wall, and from behind this the girl produced a sharp sheep shears. In a matter of moments she had the wool shorn from the pelt and, handing him the pelt, she paid him the value of the wool.

Most men would have been dumbfounded in a situation like this, and the Gobán Saor's son was no different. Nevertheless, it was with a light heart that he returned to his father's house, and tossed the shorn skin on the rail of the foot-bridge which crossed the moat.

'Well done, son,' the Gobán commended him. 'But tell me who was the sensible girl who bought the wool.'

'She's a widow's daughter from the near side of Lisgoold, father, and as fine a looking girl as ever you laid eyes on,' he told him.

'And the sort of girl that would be capable of keeping a good house for a man,' the Gobán finished.

Next morning the Gobán Saor announced an occasion of feasting for a particular day, and he issued an invitation to the widow and her three daughters. This was a rare honour so, on the appointed day, the four women from Lisgoold took their places among the poets and princes and fine ladies of the neighbourhood. The meal was a good one, with full and plenty for all, and when the meal was over, and before the music and dancing began, the Gobán called the youngest of the widow's daughters aside, and brought her into the richest room in the castle where he kept his treasure. There there were gold and silver brooches, ornamented goblets, fine tapestries, dressed furs, and many another thing to delight the heart of a girl. Over against one of the walls was a strong chest of carved oak and, lifting the cover of this, he showed her a fortune of gold pieces.

'Now, *a chroí*. What would you do with these if they were yours?' he asked her.

'Sure, indeed, I don't know what I'd do with them only to be looking at them the day long!' she told him.

'That wouldn't do at all,' he said brusquely, and he dismissed her.

Bringing in the second daughter he asked her the same question to which she replied, 'I suppose I'd just be spending it till the end of my days, what else?'

He dismissed her, too, and called in the eldest girl.

In reply to his question, she thought for a moment and said, 'I would be spending it, and adding to it!'

'Child of my heart!' he complimented her. 'Tell me

now ... how do you like that son of mine?'

She laughed that light laugh of hers and, though the red in her cheeks blushed a shade or two redder than was natural, she shrugged off her embarrassment and tossed her copper curls confidently.

'I like him fine,' she admitted, and she looked at him with steady and honest eyes.

'We'll be having a word with your mother,' he told her, and somehow he felt that here was mettle to match his own.

The wedding was a lavish affair, as all such weddings should be, and the widow was proud to have a daughter of hers married to the son of the famous Gobán Saor. The Gobán for his part welcomed his daughter-in-law into his house, and gave her full control of the establishment. She was an astute thinker, and her wise counsel was always heeded. So Rath Gobáin became a happy house once more.

One day a messenger came from Connacht saying that the king of that province intended building a strong fort and treasury in which to preserve his valuables. It was a difficult undertaking, and he wished only the best craftsmen in the country to work on it. There was no more accomplished craftsman anywhere than the Gobán Saor, so naturally there was no one more fitting to direct operations than he. The pay was rewarding, the accommodation and entertainment were of the best, would he go?

He would! How could he do otherwise in view of so flattering an invitation?

Now the son had no great regard for the king, and when he heard that his father was to make the journey to Connacht to handle the construction of this very special fort he insisted that he should accompany him. The daughter of the house was agreeable, and she made ample provisions for the road. At the moment of departure she called her husband to her.

'God be with you both on the road you go,' she prayed, 'but, remember now, there are two things you must do. You must shorten every road, and you must never sleep three nights in any house without making a friend among the ladies of the establishment. Go now with my blessing, and haste you back.'

So, mounted on two strong horses they set out on the long journey to the King of Connacht. Quietly they went at first until the Gobán Saor, noticing his son's crestfallen concentration, asked, 'What is it is disturbing you, son?'

'I'm trying to think of a way that I might shorten the road,' he said, 'and it's quite beyond me.'

The Gobán threw back his head and laughed, a hearty deep-throated laugh that echoed among the hills like thunder.

'Ah, sure, *a mhic,* isn't it you who have little sense. Can't you be telling us a story, and that will make our road short enough for anything!' And once again his laughter rang out into the valleys.

And so they went yarning from one village to the next, stopping a night here and a night there, and eventually they reached their destination at the castle of the king in Connacht. There they were received by the royal monarch himself and, while groomsmen attended to the horses, they were brought into the banqueting-hall where soon a worthy meal was served to them. Before the meal, a maid came with water and a towel for them to wash their hands. The daughter of a chief and a personal attendant on the queen, she was young and comely in appearance, and shy in the presence of the Gobán's son who was playful with her to the point of flirtation. It was the beginning of a true and highly honourable friendship which conformed to the wishes of the mistress of Rath Gobáin.

Next morning father and son inspected the ground and commenced work on the foundations of the new fort and treasure-house, and as the days went by and the walls began to rise it soon became obvious to the king and his court that here was a building the likes of which had never before been seen on top of earth. This was satisfactory in its way, but the king, a jealous, covetous soul, began to wish that no other building of its kind would ever be seen. And so it came about that, in order to procure that end, he planned to kill both the Gobán and his son when the work was completed.

One night as the work was nearing completion the young attendant to the queen was passing by the royal bedchamber when she overheard the king telling his wife of his plan to still the hands of the Munster craftsmen for ever. Horrified at the prospect she hurried to her friends' apartment and warned them of the danger threatening them. The Gobán himself was not surprised, and he acted quietly in his own wise way.

Next morning he went to the king, and said, '*A Rí*, your fort and treasure-house are all but complete, but I am ashamed to say that I have forgotten one very important tool which I need to finish the vaulting. I must go home immediately to get it.'

'Oh, my friend, that wouldn't do at all. How should I know but that some accident might befall you on the way? No, no! I will get a messenger to go,' said the king.

'Then, if I do not go my son must go,' the Gobán insisted, 'for his wife, who is now mistress at Rath Gobáin, will not give that tool into any but our own hands. Or if not to us, into the hands of anyone of royal blood who comes to her with my personal password.'

'Hmmm,' said the king doubtfully.

'As you please,' said the Gobán. 'But you must understand. This is no ordinary tool; it was worked by one of the fairy craftsmen who built the *liosanna* in my part of Munster.'

'Very well then. I will send my own son and his fosterbrother,' said the king. 'But neither you nor your son may leave the palace until your work is finished.'

The king then summoned his son to him, and commanded him to go into Munster and bring back the fairy tool. The Gobán himself advised him of the route to follow and where to rest, and he also told him the password without which he could not get the tool.

The prince and his foster-brother set out on the road early the following morning. They were mounted on the two best horses in the king's stables so that the return journey would be completed in the shortest possible time; such was the urgency of the king's necessity. The road was an easy one, and in a few days they cantered across the foot-bridge and up to the front gates of Rath Gobáin. There they were met by the mistress of the house.

Wondering at the hurry of the two men, who carried the dust of many roads on their clothes, she addressed them. 'Welcome good gentlemen, what troubles you that you ride so hard on so warm an evening?'

'We bring you greetings from the King of Connacht, our father, and a message from the Master of Rath Gobáin,' they told her. 'The Gobán Saor who has been creating a great fort for the king requests that you give us a special tool which he requires to finish the building.'

'And the name of the tool, gentlemen?'

'*Cam agus Díreach* is the password we were given,' the prince told her.

The resourceful girl pondered on these words for a moment. '*Crooked and Straight,*' she repeated to herself. She knew that no tool existed which went by such a name, so she guessed that something underhand was afoot and that, very probably, her husband and the Gobán were in danger. She reacted promptly.

'Come in, gentlemen,' she invited, and turning to one of her household she instructed that refreshments and food be brought, and that beds be prepared for the noble visitors in the Gobán's own chamber.

'You must rest with us tonight,' she said, 'and in the morning I will send you back to Connacht with the tool'

At daybreak next morning she stole to the visitors' room with six of her strongest workmen, and in a few decisive seconds they had the prince and his foster-brother securely bound. She then ordered that the prince be brought down to the deepest dungeon of the castle and, as he was being trundled into the chamber, she addressed him.

'You remain there *Cam* until *Díreach* comes!' She then locked the door, and carried away the key herself.

Back in the Gobán's chamber she told her workmen to unloose the prince's foster-brother. 'Now!' she told him. 'You will go back to your king, and tell him that his son is under lock and key in a dungeon of the Gobán Saor's castle, and that he will remain there until the Gobán and his son are conducted safely home — and that, at the latest, before the next full moon. If there is any foul play on the way he shall be put to death immediately.'

Nevertheless, she furnished him with a good breakfast and food for the road, and he, for his part, made greater haste than ever on the return journey. She then went back to the dungeon, and released the prince after he had pledged his word that he would not attempt to escape. She entertained him as befitted one of royal blood, but set a strong guard about the castle at night to ensure that neither escape nor rescue would be effected. But the prince was as honourable as the king was treacherous, and he kept his word for he, too, wished the Gobán and his son safely home.

In Connacht the king was furious and planned a big offensive against Rath Gobáin to carry away the prince by force. But the prince's mother, on hearing of it, would have none of it. She wished her son back in Connacht so she commanded the king to pay the Gobán his due, and to provide him and his son with safe conduct back to their own country.

And so, in time, the Gobán came home, and a great feast was prepared at Rath Gobáin. The prince and his retinue were treated royally, and many were the gifts they carried back to Connacht. The Gobán Saor bestowed his own personal gift upon the prince — a fine-tempered sword of his own making with a hilt of gold, a shield studded with silver, and a spear that would penetrate the hardest armour.

Such is the way of kings and courtiers.

T. CROFTON CROKER

The Banshee

The Reverend Charles Bunworth was rector of Buttevant in the County Cork about the middle of the eighteenth century. He was a man of piety and learning, and benevolent in intention. But what extended the fame of Mr. Bunworth far beyond the limits of the parishes beside his own was his performance on the Irish harp, and his hospitality to the poor harpers who travelled from house to house about the country. These itinerant minstrels sang his praises to the tinkling accompaniment of their harps, invoking in return for his bounty abundant blessings on him, and celebrating in their verses the charms of his daughters Elizabeth and Mary. Their gratitude was sincere and, at the time of his death, no less than fifteen harps had been deposited on the loft of his granary, bequeathed to him by the last members of a race which has ceased to exist.

Towards the end of his life Mr. Bunworth was taken ill. About a week before his death, early in the evening, a noise was heard at the hall door resembling the shearing of sheep, but no particular attention was paid to it at the time.

About eleven o'clock the same night Kavanagh, the herdsman, returned from Mallow whither he had been sent in the afternoon for some medicine. When he delivered the parcel to Miss Bunworth, it seemed to her that he was much agitated; at this time her father was by no means considered in danger.

'What is the matter, Kavanagh?' asked Miss Bunworth,

but the poor fellow, with a bewildered look, only uttered, 'The master, miss ... the master ... he is going from us,' and, overcome with grief, he burst into a flood of tears.

Miss Bunworth, who was a woman of strong nerve, inquired if anything he had learned in Mallow induced him to suppose that her father was worse.

'No, miss,' said Kavanagh, 'it was not in Mallow ...'

'Kavanagh,' said Miss Bunworth, 'I fear you have been drinking which, I must say, I did not expect at such a time as the present, when it was your duty to have kept yourself sober. I thought you might have been trusted. What should we have done if you had broken the medicine bottle or lost it? The doctor said it was of the greatest consequence that your master should take it tonight. But I shall speak to you in the morning, when you are in a fitter state to understand what I say.'

Kavanagh looked at her with a stupidity of aspect which did not serve to remove the impression of his being drunk, as his eyes appeared heavy and dull after the flood of tears. But his voice was not that of an intoxicated person.

'Miss,' said he, 'as I hope to receive mercy hereafter, neither bit nor sup has passed my lips since I left this house. But the master ...'

'Speak softly,' said Miss Bunworth. 'He sleeps, and is going on as well as we could expect.'

'Praise be to God for that, anyway!' replied Kavanagh. 'But, oh! miss, he is going from us surely ... we will lose him, the master, we will lose him!' And he wrung his hands together.

'What is it you mean, Kavanagh?' asked Miss Bunworth.

'The Banshee has come for him, miss,' said Kavanagh, 'and 'tis not myself alone who has heard her.'

'The banshee? An idle superstition!' said Miss Bunworth.

'Maybe so,' replied Kavanagh, 'maybe so. But as I

came through the glen of Ballybeg she was along with me, *caoining* and screeching and clapping her hands, by my side every step of the way, with her long white hair falling about her shoulders. And I could hear her repeat the master's name every now and then, as plain as ever I heard it. When I came to the old abbey she parted from me there, and turned into the pigeon field next the burying ground, and folding her cloak about her down she sat under the tree that was struck by the lightning, and began *caoining* so bitterly that it went through my heart to hear it.'

'Kavanagh,' said Miss Bunworth, who had listened attentively to this remarkable relation, 'my father is, I believe, better. Nevertheless, I charge you not to mention what you have told me, for there is no occasion to frighten your fellow servants with the story.'

Mr. Bunworth gradually declined, but nothing particular occurred until the night previous to his death. That night both his daughters, exhausted with continued attendance and watching, were prevailed upon to seek some repose, and an elderly lady, a near relative and friend of the family, remained at the bedside of their father. The old gentleman then lay in the parlour, and the head of his bed was placed close to the window. In a room adjoining sat some male friends, and in the kitchen many of the followers of the family had assembled.

The night was serene and moonlit. The sick man slept, and nothing broke the stillness of their melancholy watch until the little party in the room adjoining the parlour, the door of which stood open, was suddenly roused by a sound at the window near the bed. A rose-tree which grew outside, so close as to touch the glass, was forced aside, and a low moaning was heard, accompanied by clapping of hands, as if of a female in deep affliction. It seemed as if the sound proceeded from a person holding her mouth close to the window.

The lady who sat beside the bedside of Mr. Bunworth

went into the adjoining room, and in a tone of alarm inquired of the gentlemen there if they had heard the Banshee. Two of them, sceptical of supernatural appearances, rose hastily and went out to discover the cause of these sounds which they, too, had distinctly heard. They walked all around the house, examining every spot of ground, particularly near the window from where the voice had emanated. The bed of earth in which the rose-tree was planted had been recently dug, and the print of a footstep, if the tree had been forced aside by mortal hand, would have inevitably remained. But they could perceive no such impression, and an unbroken stillness reigned without. They continued their search along the road which was straight and lightsome, but all was silent and deserted. and they returned disappointed.

On their return to the house they were astonished to learn that, the whole time of their absence, those who remained within the house had heard the moaning and clapping of hands even louder and more distinct than before they had gone out.

Every succeeding hour the sick man became worse and, when the first glimpse of the morning appeared, Mr. Bunworth expired.

T. CROFTON CROKER

The Legend of Bottle Hill

It was in the good old days when the little people were
more frequently seen than they are in these unbelieving
times that a farmer named Mick Purcell rented a few
acres of barren ground in the neighbourhood of Mourne
Abbey, about three Irish miles from Mallow and thirteen
from the city of Cork.

Mick had a wife and family, but none of the children
was big enough to help him in his work, and it gave
the poor woman all she could do to mind the children,
milk the one cow, boil the potatoes and carry the eggs
to market at Mallow. 'Twas hard enough on them to
pay the rent betimes, but manage it they did for a time.
Then there came a bad year. The little grain of oats
was all spoiled, the chickens died of the pip, the pig
got the measles, and poor Mick found that he hadn't
enough to half pay the rent — and two gales were due.

'Why then, Molly,' said Mick, 'what'll we do?'

'Wisha, then, *mo mhúirnín*, what would you do but
to take the cow to the fair of Cork and sell her?' said
she. 'Monday is fair day, and so you must go tomorrow
so that the poor beast may be rested before the fair.'

'And what will we do when she's gone?' said Mick
sorrowfully.

'Never the know I know, Mick, but sure God won't
let us down.'

About twelve o'clock the next day he left her, with
a warning not to sell the cow except for the highest penny.
Mick promised to mind it, and went his way along the
road.

It was a fine day and the sun shone brightly on the walls of the old abbey as he forded the stream under them. He then crossed an extensive mountain tract, and after three long miles he came to the top of the hill that is now called Bottle Hill — though that was not the name of it then. Just there a man overtook him.

'Good morrow,' said he.

'Good morrow, kindly,' said Mick, looking at the stranger.

He was a small man with a bit of an old wrinkled yellow face, for all the world like a dried cauliflower. He had a sharp little nose, and red eyes and white hair. But his lips were not red, for all his face was the one colour. His eyes were never quiet, but kept looking at everything, and though they were red they made Mick feel quite cold when he looked at them. In truth, he did not much like the little man's company, and he couldn't see one bit of his legs nor his body, for though the day was warm he was all wrapped up in a big great-coat.

Mick drove his cow something faster but the little man kept up with him, gliding over the rough road like a shadow, without noise or effort and, indeed, seeming not to walk like other men by putting one foot before the other. Mick's heart trembled within him, and he said a prayer to himself, wishing he hadn't come out that day.

'Where are you going with the cow, honest man?' the small man asked him.

'To the fair of Cork, then,' said Mick, trembling at the shrill and piercing tones of the voice.

'Are you going to sell her?' said the stranger.

'Why, then, what else am I going for but to sell her?'

'Will you sell her to me?'

Mick started. He was afraid to have anything to do with the little man, but he was more afraid to say no.

'What will you give for her?' he said at last.

'I'll tell you what, I'll give you this bottle,' said the little man, pulling a bottle from under his coat.

Mick looked at him and the bottle, and in spite of his terror he could not help bursting into a loud fit of laughter.

'Laugh if you will,' said the little man, 'but I tell you this bottle is better than all the money you will get for the cow in Cork — ay, better than ten thousand times as much.'

Mick laughed again. 'Do you think,' said he, 'I'm such a fool as to give my good cow for a bottle — and an empty one, too? Indeed, then, I won't.'

'You had better give me the cow, and take the bottle — you'll not be sorry for it.'

'And what would Molly say? I'd never hear the end of it. And how would I pay the rent? And what should we all do without a penny of money?'

'I tell you this bottle is better to you than money.

Take it, and give me the cow. I ask you for the last time, Mick Purcell.'

Mick started. 'How does he know my name?' thought he.

The stranger went on, 'Mick Purcell, I know you, and I have regard for you. Therefore do as I tell you, or you may be sorry for it. How do you know but your cow will die before you go to Cork?'

Mick was going to say 'God forbid!', but the little man went on, 'And how do you know but that there will be so many cattle at the fair that you will get a bad price, or maybe you might be robbed when you are coming home? But what need I talk more to you, when you are determined to throw away your luck, Mick Purcell.'

'Oh, no! I would not throw away my luck, sir,' said Mick. 'And if I was sure the bottle was as good as you say — though I never liked an empty bottle although I had drunk the contents of it — I'd give you the cow in the name ...'

'Never mind names,' said the stranger, 'but give me the cow. I would not tell you a lie. Here, take the bottle, and when you go home do what I direct exactly.'

Mick hesitated.

'Well, then, good-bye. I can stay no longer. Once more, take it and be rich. Refuse it, and beg for your life. See your children in poverty and your wife dying for want. That will happen to you, Mick Purcell!' said the little man, with a malicious grin which made him look ten times uglier than ever.

'Maybe 'tis true,' said Mick, still hesitating. He did not know what to do. He could hardly help believing the little man and, at length, in a fit of desperation he seized the bottle. 'Take the cow,' said he, 'and if you are telling a lie, the curse of the poor will be on you.'

'I care neither for your curses nor your blessings, but I have spoken truth, Mick Purcell, and that you will find tonight if you do what I tell you.'

'And what's that?' said Mick.

'When you go home, never mind if your wife is angry. But be quiet yourself and make her sweep the room clean, set the table out right, and spread a clean cloth over it. Then put the bottle on the ground, saying these words, "Bottle do your duty!", and you will see the end of it.'

'And is that all?' said Mick.

'No more!' said the stranger. 'Good-bye, Mick Purcell, you are a rich man.'

'God grant it,' said Mick, as the small man moved off, driving the cow before him. But as he turned to take the road home he could not help looking back to get a final glimpse of the purchaser of the cow. He was nowhere to be seen!

'Lord between us and harm!' said Mick. '*He* can't belong to this earth, but where is the cow?'

She, too, was gone, and Mick went homeward muttering prayers, and holding fast the bottle. He reached home in the evening, and surprised his wife who was sitting over the turf fire in the big chimney.

'Oh, Mick, are you home already? Sure you couldn't have been to Cork and back! What has happened to you? Where is the cow? Did you sell her? What news have you? Tell us everything.'

'Why, then, Molly, if you'll give me time I'll tell you all about it. If you want to know where the cow is, 'tisn't Mick can tell you, for the never a know does he know where she is now.'

'Oh, then, you sold her! And where's the money?'

'Arrah! Stop awhile, Molly, and I'll tell you all about it.'

'But what is that bottle under your waistcoat?' said Molly, spying its neck sticking out.

'Why, then, be easy now, can't you,' said Mick, 'till I tell it to you ... that,' putting the bottle on the table, 'that's what I got for the cow!'

His poor wife was thunderstruck.

'And what good is that, Mick? Oh, I never thought you were such a fool. What will we do for the rent, and what ...?'

'Now, Molly,' said Mick, 'can't you hearken to reason? Didn't I tell you how the little man, or whatsomever he was, met me — no, he did not meet me neither, but he was there with me — on the big hill, and how he made me sell him the cow, and told me the bottle was the only thing for me.'

'Yes, indeed, the only thing for you, you fool,' said Molly, seizing the bottle to hurl it at her poor husband's head. But Mick caught it, quietly loosened his wife's grasp and placed the bottle again in his pocket.

Poor Molly sat down crying, while Mick told her his story. But as she listened she could not help believing him, particularly as she had as much faith in the fairies as she had in the priest. So she got up without saying one word and began to sweep the earthen floor with a bunch of heath. Then she tidied up everything, put out the long table and spread the clean cloth upon it.

Then Mick, placing the bottle on the ground, looked at it and said, 'Bottle, do your duty!'

'Look there! Look there, mammy!' said their chubby eldest son, a boy about five years old. 'Look there! Look there!' and he sprang to his mother's side as two tiny little fellows rose like light from the bottle and in an instant covered the table with dishes and plates of gold and silver, all full of the finest victuals that ever were seen. When all was done they went into the bottle again.

Mick and his wife looked at everything with astonishment. They had never seen such plates and dishes before, and didn't think they could ever admire them enough. The very sight almost took away their appetites, but at length Molly said, 'Come and sit down, Mick, and try and eat a bit. Sure you ought to be hungry after such a good day's work.'

'Why, then, the man told me no lie about the bottle.' Mick and his wife sat down with the children, and they made a hearty meal though they couldn't eat half the dishes.

'Now,' said Molly, 'I wonder will those two good little gentlemen carry away these fine things again.' They waited, but no one came, so Molly put away the dishes and plates very carefully, saying, 'Why, then, Mick, that was no lies sure enough. You'll be a rich man yet, Mick Purcell.'

Mick and his wife and children went to their beds, not to sleep but to discuss the selling of the fine things they did not want, and the getting of more land. Mick went to Cork, sold his plate, and bought a horse and cart.

It soon became clear that he had made money and though they did all they could to keep the bottle secret, the landlord found it out. He came to Mick one day and asked him where he got all the money, and he bothered him so much that at last Mick told him about the bottle. The landlord offered him a deal of money for it, to no avail. At last he offered to give him all his farm for ever, so Mick, who was now so rich that he thought he'd never want for money ever again, gave him the bottle.

But Mick was mistaken. He and his family spent the money as if there was no end to it and, to make a long story short, they became poorer and poorer till, at last, they had nothing left but one cow. So once more Mick drove his cow before him to sell her at Cork fair, hoping to meet the old man and get another bottle.

It was hardly daybreak when he left home, and he walked on at a good pace till he reached the big hill. The sun rose on his left and, just as he reached the summit and cast his eyes over the extensive prospect before and around him, he was startled and rejoiced by the same well-known voice.

'Well, Mick Purcell, I told you you would be a rich man.'

'Indeed, then, sure enough I was, that's no lie for you.

Good morning to you, but it is not rich I am now — but have you another bottle, for I want it now as much as I did long ago? So if you have it, friend, here is the cow for it.'

'And here is the bottle,' said the little man smiling. 'You know what to do with it.'

'Oh, then, sure I do.'

'Well, farewell for ever, Mick Purcell. I told you you would be a rich man.'

'And good-bye to you,' said Mick, as he turned back, 'and good luck to you, and good luck to the big hill — Bottle Hill it should be called — good-bye, friend, good-bye.'

Mick walked back as fast as he could, never looking back after the white-faced little gentleman and the cow, so anxious was he to bring home the bottle. He arrived with it safely enough, and called out as soon as he saw Molly, 'I've another bottle!'

'Arrah, then, you're a lucky man, Mick Purcell, that's what you are.'

In an instant she had put everything right, and Mick, looking at the bottle, exultingly cried out, 'Bottle, do your duty!'

In a twinkling, two great stout men with big cudgels issued from the bottle, and belaboured poor Mick and his wife and all his family till they lay on the floor. Then in they went again.

As soon as he recovered, Mick got up and looked around him. He thought and thought, and at last, leaving his wife and children to recover as well as they could, he took the bottle under his coat and went to his landlord who was entertaining a great company. He got a servant to tell him he wanted to speak to him, and at last he came out to Mick.

'Well, what do you want now?'

'Nothing, sir, only I have another bottle.'

'Oh, ho! Is it as good as the first?'

'Yes, sir, and better. If you like I will show it to you

100

before all the ladies and gentlemen.'

'Come along then!'

Mick was brought into the great hall, where he saw his old bottle standing high up on a shelf.

'Now,' said his landlord, 'show us your bottle.'

Mick set it on the floor, and uttered the words. In a moment the landlord was tumbled on the floor. Ladies and gentlemen, servants and all were running and roaring and sprawling and kicking and shrieking. Wine cups and salvers were knocked about in every direction until the landlord called out, 'Stop those two devils, Mick Purcell, or I'll have you hanged.'

'They never shall stop,' said Mick, 'till I get back my own bottle that I see up there at the top of that shelf.'

'Give it down to him, give it down to him before we are all killed!' said the landlord.

Mick put the old bottle into his pocket. The two men jumped back into the new bottle, and he carried them home. He got richer and richer, and one of his sons married his landlord's only daughter. All the family prospered, and Mick and his wife lived to a ripe old age.

And what happened the magic bottle? Sad to say, at Mick's wake fighting broke out among some servants and the precious bottle was broken. But the hill is still called Bottle Hill and so it will be until the end of time.

And so it ought, for it is a strange story.

T. CROFTON CROKER

The Field of Buachalauns

Tom Fitzpatrick was the eldest son of a comfortable farmer who lived at Ballincollig. He was as clever, clean, tight-limbed and good-looking a boy as any in the whole County Cork, and he was just turned of nine and twenty when he had the following adventure.

One fine day at harvest time — actually it was Lady Day, one of the greatest holidays in the year — Tom was taking a ramble through the farm. He sauntered along the sunny side of a hedge, thinking to himself where would be the great harm if people, instead of idling and going about doing nothing, were to shake out the hay, and bind and stook the oats that were lying on the ledge, especially as the weather had been rather broken of late, when all of a sudden he heard a clacking sort of noise a little before him in the hedge.

'Dear me,' said Tom, 'but isn't it really surprising to hear the stonechats singing so late in the season?'

So on he stole, rising on the tips of his toes to try if he could get a sight of whatever was making the noise, and to see if he was right in his guess. The noise stopped, but as Tom looked sharply through the bushes what should he see in a nook of the hedge but a brown pitcher that might hold about a gallon and a half of liquor. Then a teeny-weeny bit of an old man, with a little cocked hat on the top of his head and a tiny leather apron hanging before him, pulled out a little wooden stool, and stood up on it. He dipped a little *piggin* into the pitcher and took out the full of it. Then he put it beside the stool, sat down under the pitcher, and began to work

102

at putting a heel-piece on a bit of a brogue which looked
as if it would just fit himself.

'Well, by the powers!' said Tom to himself. 'I often
heard tell of the *cluricaune,* and I never rightly believed
in them. But here's one of them in real earnest! If I
go knowingly to work I'm a made man. They say a body
must never take their eyes off them or they'll escape.'

Tom stole on a little further, his eye fixed on the little
man just as a cat does with a mouse, and when he got
up quite close to him he said, 'God bless your work,
neighbour.'

The little man raised up his head, and replied, 'Thank
you kindly.'

'I wonder you'd be working on the holiday,' said Tom.

'That's my own business, not yours,' was the reply.

'Well, maybe you'd be civil enough to tell us what

103

you've got in the pitcher there,' said Tom.

'That I will, with pleasure. It's good beer.'

'Beer!' exclaimed Tom. 'Thunder and fire, where did you get it?'

'Where did I get it, is it? Why, I made it. And what do you think I made it of?'

'Devil a one of me knows,' said Tom, 'but of malt, I suppose, what else?'

' 'Tis there you're out. I made it of heath.'

'Of heath?' Tom burst out laughing. 'Sure you don't think me to be such a fool as to believe that?'

'As you please,' said the *cluricaune* 'but what I tell you is the truth. Did you ever hear tell of the Danes?'

'That I did,' said Tom. 'But what about them?'

'Well, here's what about them ... when they were here they taught us to make beer out of the heath, and the secret has been in my family ever since.'

'Will you give a body a taste of your beer?' said Tom.

'I'll tell you what it is, young man. It would be fitter for you to be looking after your father's property than to be bothering decent quiet people with your foolish questions ... there now, while you're idling away your time here, the cows have broken into the oats and are knocking the corn all about.'

Tom was so taken by surprise at this piece of information that he was just on the very point of turning around when he recollected himself. So, afraid that the like might happen again, he made a grab at the *cluricaune* and caught him up in his hand. In his hurry he overset the pitcher and split all the beer, so that he could not get a taste of it to tell what sort it was. He then swore what he would not do to the little fellow if he did not show him where his money was. Tom looked so wicked and so bloody-minded that the *cluricaune* was quite frightened, and said, 'Come along with me a couple of fields off, and I'll show you a crock of gold.'

So they went, and Tom held his captive fast in his hand and never took his eyes off him, though they had to cross hedges and ditches and a crooked bit of bog, for the *cluricaune* seemed, out of pure mischief, to pick out the hardest and most contrary way.

At last they came to a great field all full of the *buachalaun bwee*, the ragweed, and the *cluricaune* pointed to a big *buachalaun*, and said he, 'Dig under that *buachalaun*, and you'll get the great crock all full of guineas.'

Now, Tom's spade was down in the farmyard but, before running off to fetch it, he remembered to mark the spot where the gold was, and tied his garter around the *buachalaun*.

'I suppose,' said the *cluricaune* very civilly, 'you have no further occasion for me?'

'No,' said Tom, 'you may go away now. God speed you, and may good luck attend you wherever you go.'

'Well, good-bye to you, Tom Fitzpatrick,' said the *cluricaune*, 'and much good may it do you with what you'll get.'

So Tom ran for dear life, got the spade, and then back with him, as hard as he could go, to the field of *buachalauns*. But when he got there ... lo and behold! There was not a *buachalaun* in the field but had a red garter, the very identical model of his own, tied about it. It was out of the question to dig the whole field, for there were more than forty good Irish acres in it, so Tom went home again with his spade on his shoulder, and many's the hearty curse he gave the *cluricaune* every time he thought of the neat turn he had served him.

JAMES LYONS

The White Lady of Charles Fort

The imposing bulk of Charles Fort stands upon high cliffs overlooking the harbour at Kinsale, commanding the whole estuary of the Bandon River from the Old Head of Kinsale to the town. It figured in many important episodes of history, from the time of its construction in the year 1677 until its destruction about 1922. Today it is chiefly remembered because of the legend of the White Lady.

The fort is a pleasant place to spend a sunny afternoon in the height of summer, for its long grassy corridors lead among the ruined barrack buildings to stone stairways that climb on to the bastions and battlements. Derelict storehouses and dark dungeons lurk under the shadow of the walls, but the walls themselves, wide as a city street, are as airy and relaxing as a ship's deck.

About two hundred years ago, a Colonel Warrender was governor of the fort. He had a beautiful daughter who became engaged to an officer of the company, and the wedding was held in the Governor's house. During the festivities, bride and groom withdrew from the guests for a time, to take a stroll together in the afternoon sunshine on the western fortifications. They climbed one of the flights of wide steps, and stood upon the walls for a time gazing out over the harbour. Away on their left beyond the cliffs was the open ocean, on their right the town of Kinsale, cosily nestling in a deep coom at the water's end. The old fort of Castlepark was directly across the estuary, and beyond it the Bandon River shone like pond-water among the hills.

The young lovers, enjoying every beauty of the scene around them, started walking, slowly, towards the seaside turrets. There they paused again, and the bride, looking away down to the rocks below, admired some flowers that were growing there.

A sentry was on duty on a nearby turret, and in response to the officer's request he left his post to gather the flowers for the bride. The officer himself, donning the army greatcoat, stood in for the sentry and took up the watch.

Time passed tediously while they waited for the sentry to return and the bride returned to the reception party. At sundown the Governor came around to inspect the sentry posts. He found the officer asleep and, not recognising him, shot him dead on the spot.

When the sentry returned with the flowers, the tragedy was discovered. News of it soon reached the bride. She ran in a delirium from the company, on to the bastions, and at the point where she had last spoken to her lover she leaped on to the wall and then threw herself headlong into the sea.

From that day the White Lady, in her bridal gown, has haunted the Governor's house and the bastions of Charles Fort. She has been seen on numerous occasions by soldiers stationed in the Fort and the turret where the tragedy occurred is still known as the White Lady's Turret.

T. CROFTON CROKER

Teigue of the Lee

'I can't stop in this house! I won't stop in it for all the money that is buried in the old castle of Carrigrohane! If ever there was such a thing in the world — to be abused to my face night and day, and not to know who's doing it! And then, if I'm angry, to be laughed at with a great roaring, "Ho, ho, ho!" I won't stay in the house after tonight, even if there is not another place in the country to put my head under.'

This angry soliloquy was uttered in the hall of the old manor-house of Carrigrohane by John Sheehan. John was a new servant. He had only been three days in the house, which had the reputation of being haunted, and in that short space of time he had been abused and laughed at by a voice which sounded as if a man was speaking with his head in a cask. He could not discover who the speaker was nor from whence the voice came.

'I'll not stop here,' said John, 'and that ends the matter.'

'Ho, ho, ho!' said the mysterious voice. 'Be quiet, John Sheehan, or else worse will happen to you!'

John instantly ran to the hall window, as the words seemed to him to be spoken by a person immediately outside, but no one was visible. He had scarcely placed his face at the pane of glass when he heard another loud, 'Ho, ho, ho!' as if behind him. As quick as lightning he turned his head, but no living thing was to be seen.

'Ho, ho, ho, John!' shouted the voice, which now appeared to come from the lawn before the house. 'Do you think you'll see Teigue? Oh, never as long as you live! So leave off looking for him and mind your business.

There's plenty of company to dinner from Cork to be here today, and 'tis time you had the cloth laid.'

'Lord bless us! That's more of it. I won't stay another day here,' repeated John.

'Hold your tongue, and play no tricks on Mr. Pratt, as you did on Mr. Jervis about the spoons.'

John Sheehan was confounded by this address from his invisible persecutor, but nevertheless he mustered courage enough to say, 'Who are you? Come here and let me see you if you are a man.'

But he received in reply only a laugh of unearthly derision, which was followed by a 'Good-bye — I'll watch you at dinner, John!'

John had pretty well recovered himself by dinner time. Several guests arrived and they were soon seated at the table, but scarcely had they begun to enjoy the meal when a voice was heard on the lawn.

'Ho, ho, ho, Mr. Pratt, won't you give poor Teigue some dinner? Ho, ho, a fine company you have there, and plenty of everything that's good. Sure, you won't forget poor Teigue?'

'Who is that?' asked Mr. Pratt's brother, an officer of the artillery.

'That is Teigue,' said Mr. Pratt, laughing. 'You must have heard me mention him.'

'And pray, Mr. Pratt,' enquired another gentleman, 'who is Teigue?'

'That is more than I can tell. No one has ever been able to catch even a glimpse of him. I have been on the watch for a whole evening with three of my sons, yet, although his voice sometimes sounded almost in my ear, I could not see him. He visits us occasionally, and sometimes a long interval passes between his visits, as in the present case. It is now nearly two years since we heard that hollow voice outside the window. He has never done any injury that we know of, and once when he broke a plate he brought one back exactly like it.'

'How extraordinary!' exclaimed several of the guests.

'But,' remarked a gentleman to young Mr. Pratt, 'your father said he broke a plate. How did he get it without your seeing him?'

'When he asks for some dinner we put it outside the window and go away. Whilst we watch he will not take it, but no sooner have we withdrawn than it vanishes.'

'How does he know that you are watching?'

'That's more than I can tell, but he either knows or suspects. One day my brothers and I were in our back parlour which has a window into the garden. He came outside and said, "Ho, ho, ho! Masters James and Robert and Henry, give poor Teigue a glass of whiskey." James went out of the room, filled a glass with whiskey, vinegar, and salt, and brought it to him. "Here, Teigue," said he, "come for it now." "Put it down on the step outside the window," he was told.

'This was done, and we stood looking at it. "Ho, ho! you are watching Teigue! Go out of the room now, or I won't take it." We went outside the door for a few minutes and then returned. The glass was gone, and a moment after we heard Teigue roaring and cursing frightfully. The next day the glass was on the stone step under the window, and there were crumbs of bread in the inside, as if he had put it in his pocket. From that time he was not heard till today.'

'Leave it to me!' said the colonel. 'An old soldier has the best chance. I'll be ready for him when he speaks next. Mr. Bell, will you take a glass of wine with me?'

'Ho, ho! Mr. Bell,' shouted Teigue. 'Ho, ho! Mr. Bell, you were a Quaker long ago, a pretty Quaker you were, and now you're no Quaker nor anything else! Ho, ho, Mr. Bell! And there's Mr. Parkes! To be sure, Mr. Parkes looks mighty fine today with his powdered head and his grand silk stockings and his brand new rakish-red waistcoat. And there's Mr. Cole! Did you ever see such a fellow? A pretty company you've brought together, Mr. Pratt! Kiln-drying Quakers, butter-buying buckeens from Mallow Lane, and a drinking excise man from the Coal Quay — to meet the great thundering artillery-general that is come out of the Indies and is the biggest dust of them all.'

'You scoundrel!' exclaimed the colonel. 'I'll make you show yourself,' and snatching up his sword he sprang out of the window on to the lawn. In a moment laughter, so hollow, so unlike any human sound, made him stop.

'Ho, ho, Colonel Pratt! What a pretty soldier you are to draw your sword upon poor Teigue who never did anybody harm.'

'Let us see your face, you scoundrel,' said the colonel.

'Ho, ho, ho! Look at me, look at me! Do you see the wind, Colonel Pratt? You'll see Teigue as soon, so go in and finish your dinner.'

'If you're upon the earth I'll find you, you villain!' said the colonel, whilst the same unearthly shout of derision seemed to come from behind the building.

He followed the sound which was continued at intervals along the garden wall, but could find no human being. At last he stopped to draw breath, and in an instant, almost at his ears, sounded the shout, 'Ho, ho, ho, Colonel Pratt! Do you see Teigue now? Do you hear him? You're a fine colonel to follow the wind. Follow me if you can — you a soldier, ho, ho, ho!'

The colonel was enraged. He followed the voice over hedge and ditch, alternately laughed at and taunted until, after being led a weary chase, he found himself at the top of the cliff over that part of the River Lee which, from its great depth and the blackness of its water, has received the name of Hell-hole. Here, on the edge, stood the colonel, out of breadth and mopping his forehead with his handkerchief, while the voice, which now seemed close at his feet, dropped to a mocking whisper.

'Now, Colonel Pratt, if you're a soldier, here's a leap for you! Come along — look at Teigue. Ho, ho, ho! You're warm, I'm sure, Colonel Pratt, so come in and cool yourself. Teigue is going to have a swim!'

The voice seemed to be descending amongst the trailing

ivy and brushwood which clothes this picturesque cliff from top to bottom, yet it was impossible that any human being could have found footing there.

'Now, Colonel, have you courage to take the leap? Ho, ho, ho! What a pretty soldier you are. Good-bye! I'll see you again in ten minutes above at the house. Look at your watch, Colonel. There's a dive for you,' and a heavy plunge into water was heard.

The colonel stood still but no sound followed, and he walked slowly back to the house, which was not quite half a mile from the cliff.

'Well, did you see Teigue?' said his brother, whilst his nephews, smothering their laughter, stood by.

'Give me some wine,' said the colonel, 'for I never was led such a dance in my life. The fellow carried me all round and round till he brought me to the edge of the cliff, and then down he went into Hell-hole, telling me he'd be here in ten minutes. 'Tis more than that now, but he's not come.'

'Ho, ho, ho, colonel! Isn't he here? Teigue never told a lie in his life. But Mr. Pratt, give me a drink and my dinner, and then good-night to you all, for I'm tired — and that's the colonel's doing.'

A plate of food was ordered, and it was placed by John on the lawn under the window. Everyone kept on watch, and the plate remained undisturbed for some time.

'Ah, Mr. Pratt, will you starve Teigue? Make everyone go away from the windows, and order Master Henry out of the tree, and Master Richard off the garden wall.'

The eyes of the company were momentarily turned to the tree and the garden wall.

'Ho, ho, ho! Good luck to you, Mr. Pratt. 'Twas a good dinner, and there's the plate, ladies and gentlemen. Good-bye to you, colonel! Good-bye to you all.'

The plate was lying on the grass, but Teigue's voice was heard no more that evening. He paid many a visit after that, but never was he seen, nor was any discovery ever made of his person or character.

JAMES LYONS

The Fairy Herds of Blarney

An American sat in a corner near the window of the lounge of the Muskerry Hotel at Blarney in the county of Cork, alternately reading a tourist brochure and studying a map which he had spread before him on a table. The westering sun was filtering through the trees which bounded the village green, and every now and again the man lifted his eyes from the table, and looked through the foliage in the general direction of the castle.

Three countrymen entered the lounge, sat down at the table next to his and ordered drinks. Their talk was of cattle and cattle prices, of crops and the merits of fertilizers, and the sale of farms.

In time the American addressed them. 'Excuse me! I guess you folks could tell me where I might get a line on the legends of this place.'

The three men exchanged wry glances. Then one of them, a deep-chested fellow of more than average height, with round freckled face and eyes dancing under a harvest of golden hair, laughed. There was no mockery in that laugh, but one could not but suspect a certain devilment in the high-pitched trill of it.

'Ayra, man alive, is it legends you're after?' he asked, and then changing his tone to express affected sadness he continued, 'Ah sure, sorra a one we've got left. No one believes in them any more.' And again he laughed that impish laugh of his.

'But it says in this little book that the place fairly bristles with legends,' the American insisted.

'Ah, but that was long ago,' explained a second man

reasonably, 'we don't pay attention to those old stories any more.'

'You don't?' said the American, disappointed.

'Is that so?' interrupted a small dark man who had been sitting in a corner. 'And what about Nan Collins who used to live up beyond Waterloo? She put her babby in its pram outside the porch one sunny morning in the month of May, and when her back was turned the fairies carried away the child, and left a sickly changeling in its place. It died six weeks after that. Didn't I often hear my gran'ma telling the story, and gran'ma was Nan's godchild?

'And,' he continued, 'didn't you ever hear tell of Dinny Jack up at Coolowen? Without eggs for a month until a weasel came in and killed a small little black rat that had been eating the eggs from under the hens? The whole parish admitted that that was no ordinary rat. And you yourself should be the last to doubt it, Teigh Carty!' he finished, turning to the tall man.

'There never was such a thing,' Teigh repeated.

'Was there not?' the other insisted. 'And how is it your own cow above at Bawnafinne cannot produce a calf that'll live longer than a fortnight? Answer me that!'

Teigh looked at him with those steadfast eyes of his. The small dark man never flinched, and Teigh felt his own flesh creep along his spine, for it was only the other day that he had again lost a calf. He got up from the table, leaving his drink untouched, and walked firm-footed out of the lounge, slapping his payment on the bar counter as he went.

The sun had already set when he came out on to the street. He turned left along the side of the green, and walked out along the Killard road. Passing the gates of the estate he looked up the long drive at the battlements of the old castle which towered above the woodlands. Teigh's ancestors had possessed that pile, and lorded it over Muskerry for centuries but, now unhonoured, *he* farmed a few acres on the uplands westward, while the

114

castle was widely known to millions throughout the world
who, at some time or another, had come in search of
the gift of eloquence, the reward for kissing the Blarney
Stone.

Legends! Leprachauns! Jack the Lanterns! Crocks of
fairy gold! Lone bushes! No wonder he was cynical. He
had lived all of forty years, man and boy, on this land;
was bred in blood and bone out of the land; and never
as much as one small *cluricaune* had crossed his path
or tossed a golden guinea on his mantelpiece. And yet
this very day it had been suggested to him that he was
keeping a bewitched beast in rich pasture on his own
land.

'By heaven, I'll prove it otherwise,' he swore aloud

out of his thoughts, 'even if I have to drag Cliodhna herself from the rocks at Beeing to wipe her kisses from the Blarney Stone.'

Teigh had been walking hard to keep time with his thoughts, and he had become quite unmindful of the direction he was taking. He had intended calling to a friend at Killard, but never reached there. Somewhere, as the dusk was deepening, he had left the road and followed a narrow path by the side of a wood. That wood he should have known but tonight it had a strangely unfamiliar air. In depth it was insignificant, a mere fifty trees breadth at its widest point, but it extended for miles among the hills, like a vast army marching, and it bounded his own lands at Bawnafinne which were still a long way away.

That path by the wood dipped into hollows and climbed over hillocks, but always the trend was upland, and it was while he was crossing the ground above the Blarney lake that he swore his brave swear.

'By heaven, I'll prove it otherwise!'

'Sheath your sword, cousin!' A deep voice addressed him out of the shadow of the wood. 'Do not excite yourself about things you do not understand.'

Teigh stopped abruptly, startled out of his reverie, and his right hand promptly crossed in front of his stomach to his left hip-bone as if, indeed, he were gripping the hilt of a sword.

'Who's there?' he demanded, peering into the shadows.

'Have no fear, cousin, I am your friend,' the voice replied, and a warrior on horseback came forward on to the path. 'You are piqued by the loss of a new calf. Have done with it! Only do now as I tell you. Two nights from now, on the eve of Beltane, on the stroke of midnight drive your cow on to yonder pasture beside the lake, and return home immediately. Keep your eyes on the road before you. Take care not to see, nor to be seen.'

No further word was spoken. Horse and horseman

melted into the shadows, and Teigh was alone once more upon the path. He looked about him. The moon had risen, and its wan light slanted downhill across the field revealing every contour. Nothing stirred, and he felt strangely forlorn as one does when awakened from a dream. He had no idea of how he had come to be in that place at that time of night but, having got his bearings, he tarried no longer but hurried the half-mile home.

Two nights later, on the stroke of midnight, Teigh drove his cow, as he had been bidden, on to pasture beside the Blarney lake, and there he left her. He looked neither to left nor right on his way home, but kept his eyes glued to the path before him as if he were looking for something he had lost. But his thoughts were busy. He knew something of the legend of the lake behind him — and why wouldn't he, with the name he bore. For centuries it had been believed that the last ruling chief of Muskerry had hidden the family plate and treasure in or under or close to that lake, that the secret was ever held only by three living members of the family, and would continue to be passed on in this way until such time as the MacCarthys ruled again at Blarney. It was part of the legend that the chief himself visited his territory once every seventh year to patrol his land and check that all was still secure. There was also a story, and he pondered on it now, that milkers going about their work early on the morning of May Day had seen fairy herds grazing along the margin of the lake.

Teigh had never given much thought to these tales, classing them as superstition and nothing more. He lived by his beliefs, never worrying where he went at night, whether by churchyard or fairy fort or haunted derelict ruin. But tonight he was beginning to doubt his own scepticism. Who was the man who had spoken to him beside the wood two nights ago if not MacCarthy himself? He had got no very clear view of the man but, in a vague way, he imagined he had been clothed in ancient fashion, that he had spoken of a sword, and had called him cousin. The voice was unknown to him — and he knew every man's voice in the parish of Blarney. And then there were those strange instructions which he had been given and upon which he had now acted.

'You're a damn fool, Teigh Carty,' he told himself, 'to be taking notice of country tales, but as the man said — maybe you shouldn't be exciting yourself about things you don't understand.'

He went to bed as soon as he got home but remained awake for quite a while, worrying about his little cow all by her lonesome in strange pastures. She wasn't much good to him right enough, but he was fond of her and wouldn't have liked any harm to come to her. But he needn't have bothered. Having fallen asleep eventually, next morning what should he see when he looked out of the window but his wee cow grazing away happily on her own ground, the same as if she had never left it.

Time passed by, and the little cow grew stronger, and fat and glossy. Teigh was taking particular interest in her, for it seemed to him she was in calf, and that didn't make sense to him. But, sense or no sense, she eventually produced twin calves, one of them jet black like herself, the other, a bull calf, a sort of silvery-fawn, a colour the like of which he had never before seen on any animal.

Unfortunately all was not well with the little cow. She died within a fortnight and Teigh was disconsolate, for his record with calves was not good, and now he expected to be left with neither cow nor calf.

But no! The calves thrived, and out of them he built up one of the finest herds in County Cork. Exactly seven years later, to the day, the silvery-fawn bull vanished overnight, and when Teigh went into the kitchen one May morning he found a golden coin shining on his mantelpiece. It was a seventeenth-century guinea piece with the head of MacCarthy More emblazoned on it.

JAMES LYONS
The Legend of the Druid's Daughters

Cormac Mac Art, Árd Rí of Erin, was a just and able ruler who established life and law at Tara as the model for future generations. But money was needed to finance his schemes, and so tributes were levied on the provincial kings. Munster alone contributed one-fifth of the total but, because of its size and wealth, it was argued at Tara that two-fifths would be more equitable. Fiacha Muilleathan, King of Munster, refused the demand, so Cormac, acting entirely out of character, declared war on Munster. The armies of Árd Rí and provincial king clashed at Drom Domhghaire in the County Limerick.

Cormac was still a pagan, and when the tide of battle was flowing against him, as indeed it did when the determined Munstermen got moving in attack, he held a consultation with his druids who conjured up a magical trick or two. The wells and streams subsided, and soon the Munster army was without water.

Deep in the remote western fastnesses of Oileán Dairbre in Kerry dwelt Mogh Ruith, the greatest of all magicians, and to him emissaries from Fiacha were sent. His magic was greater than that of the Árd Rí's druids; he restored the water to the wells, and the final result of this battle of druidical wits was that the Árd Rí was routed and forced to abandon his claim for extra tribute.

Such was the measure of Fiacha's gratitude that he invited Mogh Ruith to forsake his Kerry retreat and promised him any land he wanted in the kingdom of Munster. The druid chose an extensive tract of lush land on the banks of the Blackwater, between the Ballyhoura hills and the Nagles mountains. To the east lay the Knockmealdowns, while westwards the rich lands of Ó Caoimh extended to the Kerry borders.

Mogh Ruith was descended from Ruaidhri Mór of Ulster, and his palace in Máigh Méine was worthy of a king. There he enjoyed life with his wife and daughters, and the girls were admired throughout the territory for their beauty and refinement. Aoevil, the younger, was open-hearted and gay, loving life and making life that little bit more lovely for those around her. Cliodhna, more inclined to stand on her dignity, commanded respect and attention rather than love. Both girls dabbled in magic, but Cliodhna was the enchantress supreme and she changed people into strange forms for fun or malice. Beautiful and seductive, she knew how to wind a man around her finger, but like many another woman before and since she carried a hard core of jealousy in her soft maidenly heart.

The gaming-greens of the palace were a venue for regular tournaments, and the clash of steel, the thunder of hooves, the encouraging cheers of spectator warriors were often heard upon the green uplands along the Blackwater. Representatives of the leading septs competed regularly and Caomh, the neighbouring chief, was ever an accomplished and admired contestant in the games. A close friendship had developed between him and the ageing druid, and the druid's daughters too were happy in his company.

One evening before sunset Mogh Ruith sat on the veranda in front of the palace, and Cliodhna was with him, standing at the balustrade facing the sun, her back to him. The greens below were trimmed in readiness for the morrow's tournament, and the low western sun cast a golden glow over the whole arena. Both were silent for a time, enjoying the warmth, and then Mogh Ruith spoke. 'What do you see in the sun, daughter?' he asked. She stirred not a muscle in her back or shoulders, but answered quietly.

The Blackwater

'I see sorrow and sin in the sun, father, and a clean blade flashing.'

'The blade we know,' the druid commented, 'and it will be forever clean. But a cloud will cover the sun, quenching the blade, and its shadow shall chill the whole plain of the Allo. What are your thoughts, daughter.'

Cliodhna turned towards him, and she stood now like a priestess in her long flowing robe with her back to the sun, motionless.

'My thoughts are of Caomh, father,' she answered him simply.

'I have noticed the velvet tone of your voice when you speak of him. Do you love him?' he asked.

'I am in love with him, father,' she admitted. 'Does it please you?'

'It does. He is a man of noble character, and I would be happy to have him for my son. Have you an understanding with him?'

'No, father, we have not spoken of it. But I do know he enjoys my friendship and company,' Cliodhna told him.

'I am sure you are right about his feelings,' the druid said. 'I must be making arrangements with him.'

'No, father! Not until I speak to him first,' Cliodhna commanded.

'As you wish,' he agreed. 'He will be at the games tomorrow.'

Caomh came and conquered. Javelin, sword, *camán*, discus, chariot — he excelled on every field, and the two daughters of the druid were foremost in their admiration. Cliodhna was restrained as was her habit, but the less inhibited Aoevil raced up to him when he came from the arena after the final competition and, throwing her arms around him, impulsively she kissed him and poured out her heart in a quick torrent of words.

'Oh, Caomh, Caomh, my champion, I love every little bit of you!' and she held him at arm's length and the two dancing eyes that looked into his were the brightest he had ever seen.

This outpouring of affection was no surprise to Caomh, for Aoevil and he had been on more than friendly terms for some time, but to Cliodhna the act of self-expression which she had witnessed came as a complete surprise. Both sisters had always been inseparable companions, but the suspicion that Aoevil might have won Caomh's love worked evil in her heart. She had not yet learned that people in love are naturally reticent, and that Aoevil had not acted secretly against her. The dormant jealousy had found an outlet at last.

Cliodhna's old nurse knew more about magic than anyone in the druid's palace, and Cliodhna turned to her in her hour of distress. The nurse's apartment was high up in a turret on the north-western corner of the palace; the only approach to it was by a narrow stone spiral stairs, so that it was virtually cut away from the rest of the building. It was pierced by three windows, one facing south-west, one north-west, one north-east, and they provided a look-out along two sides of the palace. It was a small room but bright and cheerful, and in the various nooks were collected cups of brass, bronze and nickle of various sizes. To this room Cliodhna hurried after dark and, slightly out of breath, she knocked on the strong oak door. The old nurse opened slowly, throwing a flood of candlelight on to the dark landing where the girl waited.

'Wisha, Cliodhna, *a ghrá gheal,* what brings you in such a *sodar* to poor Sadhbh so late in the night?' the old woman questioned her.

'Hush, Sadhbh! I want you to do me a favour,' and she slipped quietly inside.

'What is it, *a leanbh?'* Sadhbh wondered. 'Sit you down.'

'Do you know Caomh of Duhallow, Sadhbh?'

'I have been watching him coming and going this many a day, *a chroí.* A fine upstanding nobleman, I would say.'

'I am in love with him, Sadhbh,' Cliodhna said seriously.

'You are indeed, *a leinbhín,* but Aoevil is in love with him, too, and it's a great pity for the both of you.'

'But, Sadhbh! How did you know? I didn't know myself until after the tournament today,' Cliodhna asked in surprise.

'Ah, sure, *a chailín,* 'tis many's the thing I see from my three curious windows,' Sadhbh admitted. 'One evening and I watching the two of them laughing and playing with each other along the bridle-path, and they sharing the odd kiss in the shadow of the bushes, I said to myself — that young man will be a trouble to my little ones yet. And wasn't I right? 'Tis a hard thing, *a ghrá,* when two girls fall in love with the one man.'

Cliodhna was disturbed by this news. She had been hoping that Aoevil's recent expression of love was but a spontaneous gesture activated by Caomh's overwhelming successes at the games, but Sadhbh's disclosure suggested otherwise. She was now absolutely determined to win her own way with the chief.

'My dear Sadhbh, I love my sister as you well know, and I am greatly disturbed that this thing has come to divide us. I would not wish to injure her, but I must make her change her mind. I must have Caomh. Will you work a spell on her to make her forget?'

'Cliodhna, *a chroí,* you know spells are tricky things to be tinkering with. One small mistake can bring death. Would you wish me to endanger your sister's life? Why not let things take their course — you would both be happier for it?' the old woman advised her. 'Aoevil has no physical advantage over you. You are as clever as she is, and as attractive in your ways. Girls are always competing with each other over boys — why shouldn't you win?'

'No, no, Sadhbh! I must have help — no matter what the risk — and I depend on you.'

'Very well so,' Sadhbh agreed reluctantly. 'Come to

me again to morrow night, and I'll do my best for you.'

Sadhbh spent most of the next day walking through the palace gardens, searching for the herbs which she needed to bind the spell which would bring Caomh into the waiting Cliodhna's bower. She collected berries of the cuckoo-pint under a woody ditch, white tufts of *cannavaun* on the turfy edges of the lake, green *sceachóirí* from the lone bush near the sacred well, and other herbs whose names and uses are fortunately unknown to us today.

An hour before sunset Sadhbh retired to her turret room and prepared for the processing of each individual herb. She selected thirteen of her little metal cups, trimmed one rushlight for every cup and, at the precise moment when the reddening sun dipped below the western skyline, she set a light in position under every cup. Then she started to recite a long litany of incantations and, as she moved about the room, she attended to each cup in turn, dropping a seed into one, a berry into another, a mashed leaf into a third, and so on until something had been deposited in every cup.

Now Sadhbh was not witch-like in appearances or bearing but when, at this stage of the ritual, she donned a heel-length black cloak and cowl she seemed to change in mien and personality. There was now a cat-like cunning about her movements, as she looked into each of the cups in turn like a jackdaw peering into a chimney-pot. Around and around the room she prowled, all the time adding extra ingredients to the cups as she went.

Sometime after dark Cliodhna knocked on the door, and was admitted. A heavy bitter-sweet odour permeated the apartment. No word passed between the women, and Cliodhna sat aside feeling slightly faint and dizzy. Sadhbh completed another circuit, uttering a final spell over each cup, and she quenched the light at the end of each incantation. Finally, she did a remarkable thing. Unloosing her cloak she whirled it once at arm's height above her head, and sent it floating around the room.

Three times it circled the room, and when it landed in the centre of the floor it was like a shroud of mourning draped on a bier. Even Cliodhna was startled.

'It's an ill-omen,' Sadhbh admitted, and then, urgently, she knelt on the floor at Cliodhna's feet and held the girl's hands in her own.

'Cliodhna, *a mhúirnín,* is there nothing I can say to you to turn you aside from the thing that is in your mind?'

For long seconds the two women looked into each other's eyes — aged eyes appealing, youthful eyes shining behind a faint film of tears. Often in years gone by they had enacted scenes such as this, and always had the tears welled from Cliodhna's eyes in obedience to her nurse. But she was now a woman grown — motivated by jealousy — and the tears refused to flow. Nevertheless, there was a *tocht* in her heart when she spoke.

'I'm sorry, Sadhbh, my dear. What will be must be. I will take a chance with the syrup you have prepared.'

'Very well, *a chroí.* I will get the juices bottled, and may the great gods of Danaan guard us!'

From that day forward Aoevil's health declined, and the strained relationship between her and her sister slowly became worse. Cliodhna, for all her hard-headed pursuit of her own ambition, was deeply concerned but the old jealousy persisted.

Caomh continued to visit the palace. His affection for Aoevil, never a secret, was now strikingly evident, and Cliodhna, though she was being treated as courteously and graciously as ever, had to acknowledge her secondary role in the romantic drama. Right through Aoevil's tedious illness she acted as nurse and attendant, always with a measure of genuine sympathy and sadness for her sister in her weakness and depression. But notwithstanding she continued with the enchantment until, at the appropriate time, she administered a final draught of Sadhbh's enchanted syrup. This induced lethargy, trance, apparent death, and the deceived household was plunged into mourning for the passing of the beloved younger princess. She was waked according to custom, and entombed in a vault under the palace.

That night Cliodhna again visited Sadhbh's turret. The old lady was distressed but full of hope.

'Hurry you now, *a ghile,* and maybe this night's work will bring release to Aoevil and consolation to yourself.'

Silently and stealthily she shepherded the girl down the dark stairs into the garden, then through a secret tunnel and concealed opening into the vault in which Aoevil was entombed. Thereafter they removed her, by means known only to themselves, to a deep cave in the place which is known today as Castlecor in the barony of Duhallow. There they kept quiet watch, and with their soft and soothing talk enticed her out of her trance. Slowly, drowsily, she awakened and looked sleepily at Sadhbh; then beyond her into the shadows on the walls of the cave; and finally her gaze came to rest on Cliodhna. Recognition came — suddenly— and she leaped up throwing herself at her sister, embracing her tightly.

'Oh, Cliodhna! Cliodhna! I've had the most horrible nightmare . . . you and Sadhbh, mother, father, the whole palace weeping and I myself dead on a bier. Oh, my dear, dear sister! Hold me close to you,' and she let her head fall sobbing on Cliodhna's shoulder. 'Sadhbh,' she continued low-voiced, extending her hand to the old nurse. 'Catch my hand, Sadhbh,' but Sadhbh only turned away and withdrew into the shadows, weeping.

Aoevil continued to cry as though her heart must break, and Cliodhna herself was so moved to pity that she wavered in her determination to subdue her unfortunate sister. But then Aoevil controlled her emotion and, lifting her head, she looked about the cave.

'Cliodhna! Where are we?' she asked urgently.

'Hush, pet!' Cliodhna soothed her. 'You are not at the palace now, but in a place where you will be safe.'

'Oh, Cliodhna, please take me to my father. Cliodhna,

I must see Caomh. Oh, my beloved Caomh! Cliodhna! Where is Caomh? Caomh should be here. Caomh *would* be here if he knew how frightened I am. Oh, that horrible dream! Cliodhna! It was a dream, Cliodhna, wasn't it? Oh, Cliodhna, tell me 'twas a dream,' and almost in hysterics she looked up into Cliodhna's cold eyes. 'Cliodhna!' she all but screamed. 'Cliodhna! Why are you looking at me like that? Oh, Cliodhna,' and slowly, broken-heartedly she said it. 'What are you doing to me?'

Cliodhna, once again consumed with jealously on hearing Caomh's name on her sister's lips, snapped a command.

'Enough, Aoevil! Renounce Caomh! He is betrothed to me, he is mine! Do you promise?'

'No, no, never!' said Aoevil through her tears. 'As long as I shall live I will love Caomh, and Caomh will love me. Oh, Cliodhna, you have done this to me. You have drawn the flesh off my bones, and I know now you want me to die. But you cannot kill my love, nor can you kill Caomh's love for me. Do your worst, that you can never do!' And she turned away from the angry Cliodhna.

'Aoevil, you will rue this night,' Cliodhna hissed. Taking her fairy wand from some inner secret fold of her garments she pointed it toward her sister while intoning some enchanted formula.

Suddenly Aoevil was changed into the form of a magnificent white cat, and the cave itself was transformed into a beautiful palace, sumptuously furnished with priceless fabrics, jewels and metals, the floor as thickly carpeted with gold and silver coins as would be a woodland glade in late October.

'Now my sister,' Cliodhna continued remorselessly. 'Here shall you reign until I release you from your enchantment — and that will only be when you have agreed to put every thought of your so beloved Caomh from your mind and heart. But for one week of every year, at midsummer, you will be privileged to assume your own natural form and if, in the course of that week, Caomh or any man seeks you and loves you for yourself alone, without coveting your riches, then too shall the enchantment be broken and you shall go free. Farewell, my sister. It is a sad day that you and I should now be parted for the love of a man.'

Caomh had been attending to his affairs at the westernmost fringes of his territory while these intrigues were being enacted in Mogh Ruith's palace, and Aoevil had already been entombed and transformed before he learned of her apparent death. It was a sad blow to Caomh, and man though he was, he wept bitter tears that his beloved princess had been taken in the bloom of her youth and beauty. His grief was great but, as he was young and resilient, it was not mortal. But sorrow weighed so heavily on the druid, and on his wife that they pined away as Aoevil did, and died in a relatively short time.

Cliodhna was now queen in her own court. Caomh was free, though a prisoner still in his thoughts as he forever sought some plausible explanation for the apparently inexplicable decline and death of the younger princess. Cliodhna watched him attentively, tenderly, always tempering her eagerness to win his affection to herself with a patience that was as prudent as it was painful to her. He visited the palace often as was to be expected, and he found pleasure and consolation in remembering Aoevil in her own environment. But Cliodhna, too, had been his friend, and while in her company he tasted something of the peace and comradeship which he had enjoyed with Aoevil.

One day the two of them sat together on the veranda, Caomh in the same seat where Mogh Ruith had rested that evening when he had read strange portents in the sun. The sun was again sinking towards the west, and

Cliodhna sitting to the side and forward was caught in the warm, alluring, honey-golden, evening glow of it. Caomh was looking out over the lush uplands as Mogh Ruith had done, but he seemed intent on some lost dream of his own and did not notice the anxious glances the girl directed toward him from time to time. Eventually it was she who broke the silence.

'Caomh, my dear, why do you not talk to me for a while? You are completely withdrawn from me ... you who used to be so easy, so gay, so debonair.'

He did not answer immediately, but sighed and smiled a wan wistful smile. Cliodhna coaxed him. 'You are thinking of Aoevil, Caomh ... always and always of Aoevil.'

'That is so,' he agreed. 'That is so,' and he lapsed into silence again.

'And yet, neither grief nor longing can bring her back to us,' Cliodhna continued. 'We used to have happy times, Caomh, when we were all together. Only we two are left, each of us sorrowing, but should we not try to salvage something of the happiness we once knew? Our grief cannot restore those who have gone from us.'

She got up from her chair, and walking to the balustrade she rested her hands on the polished rail. She looked out over the trim gardens to wide pastures beyond, and far away she saw the haze-grey mountains which bounded Caomh's territories in the west. She came back across the terrace, and sat close to the young chief, resting her two hands on the back of one of his.

'Caomh!' and her voice was like velvet in her throat, 'could not a sister's love give substance to your dreams?'

'A sweetheart's sister's love, do you mean?' he wondered wryly. 'Do not doubt that Aoevil and I loved each other always, Cliodhna, but love can overshadow love. What then?'

'Yes, Caomh, but without the substance there can be no shadow,' and she left it at that.

Cliodhna the woman had discarded her magic and

was weaving an enchantment that was purely human. In spite of her wiles and wilfulness she was very much Aoevil's sister in looks, in temperament, in tenderness, in spontaneity, and Caomh's gradually growing love for her was in no way a betrayal of Aoevil's love for him. In fact he saw it as something which would have had Aoevil's approval from beyond the grave. The sisters had been inseparable in life, and he had found companionship easy with both. In loving Cliodhna now he continued to love Aoevil, for in Caomh's life Cliodhna and Aoevil had been one in spirit with him.

Cliodhna and Caomh were married with such pomp and pageantry as normally enlivened these occasions. For Cliodhna it was the fulfilment of a deep and genuine emotion which she had nurtured honestly and pursued fairly until jealousy grew to warp her outlook. She was no longer the unscrupulous enchantress, the unashamed schemer, but a young bride full of dreams and hopes for the future. She wished above all else, and the thought was ever uppermost in her mind, that Aoevil would now be reasonable and free herself from her enchantment. But Aoevil would not. She continued to profess her love for Caomh, saying that she would not forget him as long as either of them lived. Under such a threat to her own happiness, Cliodhna knew she could not break the spell herself.

Cliodhna and Caomh lived happily together, and if Cliodhna had any qualms of conscience she did not show it. In the course of time a son, heir to their united territories, was born and he was followed, a year later, by twin girls. The family continued to grow as the years passed, and life was pleasant for parents and children.

They had three palaces in which to reside, according to mood and occasion. Two of them in Fer Máigh Féine were Cliodhna's own, and the third was Caomh's. They were staying at the druid's old palace when, inevitably, Cliodhna's past came back to haunt her. One morning as she was playing in the garden with the children a messenger came to Caomh from Sadhbh, who still occupied the turret room in the north-western corner of the building.

Sadhbh was now advanced in years. She had been ailing for some time, and had long ago given up experimenting in magic. Sometimes, indeed, her nights were fretful with thoughts of things she had attempted and achieved, and sometimes a white cat came prowling through her dreams. The animal was beautifully proportioned, with a coat that shone like silk, and it walked as gracefully as a princess at a grand ball. The eyes held no malice as a cat's eyes might, but always they looked at her with a sad reproachful look, and never yet had she heard it purr. Sometimes it mewed softly, plaintively, as it passed her, though most times it passed in silence.

Aoevil passed through her dreams at other times, and she moved with feline grace, quietly, unhurriedly. The eyes of the girl were reproachful, too, and on one occasion only did she speak, and then it was the old lady's name she called, softly, sadly — 'Oh, Sadhbh, Sadhbh!'

And so Sadhbh sent a messenger to Caomh. '*A Thíghearna!*' the boy piped excitedly as he ran into the yard where his master was running an experienced hand over a grey mare which he had just added to his stables. '*A Thíghearna,* the old nurse, Sadhbh, is taken sick and says to have you go to her without delay. 'Tis important she says.'

Caomh had a very high regard for Sadhbh so, with a quick word to the boy to put the mare in her stable, he hurried to the turret room. There he found the old lady stretched on her bed, breathing heavily.

'Oh, Caomh, *a stór,* 'tis you are kind to old Sadhbh to come so quickly. Listen to me, Caomh. I haven't much time, and I must ask you to forgive me ...' She paused a while to get her breath, and Caomh raised her into an easier position in the bed and held her with his arm supporting her back and shoulders.

'What is it I must forgive, Sadhbh, I didn't know you had done me any wrong?' he asked tenderly, reassuringly.

'Oh, I did, *a chuid,* I did ... a serious wrong, and I loving you. And I loving Aoevil. But Cliodhna had a hold on me, and I loved her, too.' Caomh was taken aback by this unexpected reference to Aoevil and Cliodhna.

'Yes, Sadhbh?' he encouraged her.

'Too much love there was in it,' she continued. 'Cliodhna was in love with you, Caomh, but she was jealous of you and Aoevil, and jealousy is the mischief. You are happy with Cliodhna now, but Aoevil is not happy. That is right, son,' she added urgently, seeing the consternation and disbelief in his eyes. 'That is right. Aoevil is not dead! She's under a spell, and I am to blame. Cliodhna persuaded me to help her put an enchantment on Aoevil so that she could have you for herself, and I was weak.'

Here the old woman closed her eyes, and was silent for some minutes, finding it hard to regain her breath after such a long speech. Caomh, for her sake, controlled the turbulent emotions which threatened to overwhelm him.

'Caomh, *a chroí,'* she continued after a while, 'what I did was to be temporary. But what Cliodhna did in anger is for ever unless you can persuade her to undo the enchantment she put on her sister after the whole country thought her dead. Listen to me now. Cliodhna transformed your sweetheart into a beautiful white cat, and she lives in a cave on the uplands of Duhallow. And 'twas myself made it possible by putting her into the trance which people thought was death.'

Again she lapsed into silence, and her tears flowed freely. 'And wasn't it because of me, indirectly, that the old druid and his good woman died? I shouldn't have given in, Caomh. I wouldn't have if I had really known the depth of Cliodhna's jealousy. Talk to her tonight. Tell her I told you about Aoevil. Tell her I begged of her to release her sister from the enchantment. Do all you can to persuade her. Caomh, my brave, generous champion! Of you I beg forgiveness. Can you forgive a poor foolish woman before she dies?'

She looked into his eyes, and there was pleading in her own.

'Oh, to think that I should have been the cause of hurting any of you, Caomh!'

'Hush, my dear, be easy,' Caomh consoled her. 'Yes, Sadhbh, I forgive you — a foolish woman as you said. But it wasn't your fault. Rest you now, *a mháthairín.*'

'Dear boy, thank you. Now they can come to me from *Tír na n-Óg,* and may Danann and his good people smile on you always and strengthen your hand.' Then, with a long contented sigh, she turned her head to rest on his shoulder and slipped easily out of life.

When Caomh left Sadhbh's apartments he hurried into the gardens to find Cliodhna. She was still sitting on the edge of the terrace watching the children at play, and Caomh's sudden arrival startled her. There were no preliminary remarks.

'Cliodhna, Sadhbh is dead. She died in my arms a few minutes ago.'

'Oh, no!' She rose to her feet, and for one short moment a hint of fear clouded her eyes. 'Sadhbh! Poor Sadhbh! But what happened, Caomh?'

'A sudden spasm ... heart,' he told her bluntly. 'She sent a messenger for me, urgently. She was afraid to die. Why should an old woman be afraid to die ... could you tell me, Cliodhna?'

'There could be many a thing on an old woman's mind,' she parried.

'Or on a young woman's,' he suggested, and his eyes held hers in their steadfast gaze.

'On a young woman's, too,' she agreed, 'though she mightn't be going to die.'

'And if she *were* going to die?' he persisted.

Cliodhna raised herself to her full height, authority in every defiant line of her as she faced him. 'Caomh! What is on your mind, husband? Don't you dare play games with me.'

'Women! One of them is dead. One of them was dead — but she lives. The third . . . what of the third, Cliodhna?'

'Why did Sadhbh send for you?'

'She wanted to ask my forgiveness for a wrong she had done me. But Sadhbh did me no wrong!'

Cliodhna was silent and Caomh continued, 'Sadhbh gave me a message also for you.'

'Yes?'

' "Tell her," she said. "Tell her I begged of her to release her sister from her enchantment." '

'Caomh! Don't you think I haven't been eating my heart out for Aoevil. I have been to see her. I would have done everything I could to restore her to her place among her people if she had been reasonable. But she has not been reasonable. Although she believes you dead . . . killed in battle as I convinced her . . . she still loves you, and . . .'

'Is it unreasonable to love me then?' he cut in.

'Unreasonable, yes, to love a dead man. And she knew I loved you before ever you showed interest in her. She wanted you, even though she knew it wounded her only sister,' Cliodhna said bitterly.

'And because she refused to give in to her sister's jealousy she had to be put under that terrible spell! Release her, and restore her to her own form — if not for her own sake, for mine whom you profess to love?'

'Caomh, darling, believe me. I would, but I have not now the power.' She paused. 'I lost my wand while we were living at your own palace seven seasons ago, and now I am helpless.'

'You mean that now — or ever — you cannot release Aoevil from the enchantment in which you have ensnared her?' Caomh asked, disbelief in his voice.

'That is so,' she told him simply.

'Then, by the power of whatever gods you serve, find yourself another husband,' and it was a very angry man indeed who left her abruptly.

Things were never the same after that for Cliodhna and Caomh. He was brusque where he had been gentle, cold where he had been affectionate, cruel where he had been considerate, deaf to her entreaties, blind to her needs, suspicious in all dealings with her, uncompromising in his demands of her, sparing of his courtesies toward her. She bore it patiently, hopefully, for a time until, eventually, she withdrew with her two daughters into the mountains south of the river, and made her palace under the grey rocks that have been known from that day forward as Carrig Chliodha.

Caomh came to visit her there, always appealing for the release of Aoevil. But Cliodhna was powerless as she said. In time, when she had educated her daughters to her own desire, she returned them to their father but he, overburdened with heavy sorrow and having lost both his loves through such curious circumstances, died soon afterwards.

Aoevil never was released from her enchantment, but continued to reign in her cave-palace which ever afterwards, and even to the present day, was known as *Poll na gCat*. Nevertheless, for one week each year she assumes her original form. Cliodhna joins her then, and there is a great hosting of fairies from the palaces of Munster. The sisters, now united by grief, rejoice in each other's company during that brief respite, then part for another year. Cliodhna rules her kingdom from the sprawling rocks of Beeing, a queen in her own right, and under the uplands of Castlecor Aoevil hopefully awaits the suitor who, spurning her wealth and loving her for herself, alone can break the snare that binds her.

But Aoevil's enchanted palace is closely guarded by the *Sídhe,* and he would be a superhuman suitor indeed who could win his way to woo her.

Notes

Crofton Croker appended copious notes to the stories he collected; I have abstracted the relevant sections. The notes for my stories are the result of my research and investigation.

Author.

The Legend of the Lough

Loch na bhFearnóg, literally 'the lake of the alders', is the topographic name of the lake which is known to all Corkonians nowadays as The Lough.

A somewhat similar legend is related by Burton in his *History of Ireland* and by Giraldus Cambrensis, but the setting is Lough Neagh in the North; Thomas Moore took it as his inspiration for the poem which begins, *On Lough Neagh's bank, as the fisherman strays . . .'*

Stories of cities and palaces beneath the waves often have a foundation in fact (a flooding or an earthquake); Crofton Croker records a peasant in the west of Ireland telling a visitor about 'a great city' which could be seen beneath the waters of a local lough.

At the banquet, the phrase 'Fresh food and the most mature of drinks' derives from an ancient Irish saying — *Nua gac bíadh, sean gac díghe* (new every food, old every drink) — which was the traditional hallmark of hospitality.

The Headless Horseman

The headless horseman is a favourite theme in folk literature. In Denmark, the *Groen Jette,* the wild huntsman, rides with his head under his arm.

The Death Coach

According to Crofton Croker, headless people were known as Dullahans — from *Dubhlachan,* a dark sullen person. 'The death-coach is called in Irish, *coach a bower.* The time of its appearance

137

is always midnight, and when heard to drive round any particular house, with the coachman's whip cracking loudly, it is said to be a sure omen of death.'

The following account of their activities was given by a Cork lady: 'They drive particularly hard wherever a death is going to take place. The people about here thought that the road would be completely worn out with their galloping before Mrs. Spiers died. On the night the poor old lady departed they brought an immense procession with them, and instead of going up the road, as usual, they turned into Tivoli: the lodge-people, according to their own account, 'were *kilt* from them that night'. The coachman has a most marvellously long whip, with which he can whip the eyes out of any one, at any distance, that dares to look at him. I suppose the reason he is so incensed at being looked at, is because he cannot return the compliment, *'pon the' count* of having no head. What a pity it is none but the Dullahans can go without their heads! Some people's heads would be no loss to them, or any one else.'

The 'whipping out of the eyes' is also recorded by Thiele in Denmark. 'The oppressive lords of Glorup drive every Christmas night, in a stately coach, from their magnificent tomb in St. Knud's Church in Odense, to Glorup. The coach is drawn by six white horses with long glowing tongues; and he who dares not hide his face when he hears it coming, atones for his rashness with loss of sight.'

The localities mentioned in the poem are all in the immediate vicinity of the city of Cork, with the exception of Schull and the Old Head of Kinsale, both of which lie on the coast.

Barry of Cairn Thierna

Crofton Croker relates how the great pile of stones on the top of Cairn Thierna came into being. O'Keefe, lord of Fermoy, had an only son of whom it was foretold that he would be drowned. Hoping to avert the doom, his father decided to build a castle on Cairn Thierna, far from lakes and rivers. Workmen were engaged to raise mighty stones from the base to the summit of the mountain. The son, wandering about the site, came across a vessel containing a small supply of water for the workmen, and never having seen water before he was attracted to it. He leaned over to investigate his own reflection and, losing his balance, the fatal prophecy was accomplished. So the unfinished castle was abandoned.

According to local tradition, the great Barry had his magic dwelling on this summit.

Another version of this story substitutes a lady for Barry and the scene is Blarney in the time of Cromwell, but the circumstances of the billet, the supper, the cow-hide and the loss of the cow are precisely similar.

Dreaming Tim Jarvis

'Lily-white thirteens' refers to the English shilling which was worth thirteen pence in Irish currency.

The notion of dreaming about treasure is also recorded in German and Danish folklore. One tragic consequence was chronicled in Ireland in 1774. A man who dreamed three times about money concealed under a large stone got some workmen to help him to move it; when they dug to the foundations it suddenly fell, killing the treasure-seeker.

Crofton Croker gives, from *Discoverie of Witchcraft*, the proper 'art and order' to be followed when digging for buried treasure.

The Forsaken Grave on Shournaghside

This is a tale which has been handed down for generations in the mid-Cork area, and is well known even in the city.

A hundred yards from the River Shournagh (pronounced Showernock), at Loughane, a little cluster of trees protects the site of an ancient church (marked on an old ordnance map in the City Library). Adjoining the trees is a field which is known as the Coffin Field. This is where the priest-slayer was buried and a stone there is said to mark his grave.

Mathey graveyard, on the top of the hill across the river, is about a mile from the Coffin Field, and even today older folk can point out the gravestones that had fallen into the river during the flight of the dead.

The soldiers probably came from Ballincollig, the military centre of the area. Fox's Bridge perpetuates the name of the villain of the piece, General Fox.

The Priest's Supper

It was a common medieval belief that elves and fairies were part of the crew that fell with Satan, but their criminality was considered less so they were visited with minor punishment and allowed to inhabit the earth. But the question of their ultimate salvation was left uncertain.

A Legend of Kilcrea Friary

This legend is recorded in the *Journal of the Cork Historical and Archaeological Society* (Vol. IIA, page 18). 'Muntervarry' derives from *Muintir Mhuire* — the people of Mary.

Kilcrea Friary was founded in 1465 by Cormac Láidir MacCarthy who was buried there in 1494 (he was murdered by his brother). Seven of his descendants, down to his great-great-grandson, are also buried there. In the choir, opposite the MacCarthy tomb, lies Dr. T. O'Herlihy, a Bishop of Ross; after his release from the Tower of London and Dublin Castle he spent some time with MacCarthy More at Macroom Castle.

Arthur O'Leary served as an officer of the Hussars in the army of Maria Therese. When he returned home the Penal Laws were in force. One law was that a Protestant was entitled to offer £5 for any horse owned by a Catholic. O'Leary had a bitter enemy named Morris, who when he was beaten by O'Leary at a race-meeting near Carrigadrohid insisted on buying the horse. O'Leary refused and was forced to become an outlaw. He was eventually ambushed and killed near Millstreet. His wife, Eibhlín Dubh Ní Chonaill, whose nephew was Daniel O'Connell, wrote a famous lament for him. Morris was later shot by O'Leary's brother who then fled to America.

The Giant's Stairs

Dr. Smith in his *History of Cork* (Vol. 1, p. 172), says: 'He (Mr. Philip Ronayne) invented a cube which is perforated in such a manner that a second cube *of the same dimensions exactly in all respects* may be passed through the same.'

Hanlon's Mill

In English folklore, King Arthur is said to hunt in the woods, invisible to all, but the sounds of horn and hounds can be heard plainly. France has a similar phantom huntsman in the Grand Veneur, who hunts around Fontainebleau.

Daniel O'Rourke

'The tale of Daniel O'Rourke, the Irish Astolpho, is a very common one, and is here related according to the most authentic version. The castle of Carrigaphouca, beneath the walls of which O'Rourke was discovered, is doubtless the one of that name situated about two miles west of Macroom.'

The Haunted Celler

Crofton Croker writes: 'The *cluricaune* of Cork, the *luricaune* of Kerry and the *lurigadaune* of Tipperary, appear to be the same as the *leprechaun* of Leinster and the *loghery* man of Ulster; these words are probably provincialisms of *luacharma'n*, the Irish for pygmy.

Naggeneen, the name of this particular *cluricaune*, implies something even less than the smallest measure of drink; a naggin being about the same as half a gill. *Een* is the Irish diminutive.'

The Spirit Horse

Ballyvourney, the town of my beloved, is about six miles west of Macroom and is regarded as a place of peculiar holiness. Crofton Croker got this description of the pooka from a local boy: 'Old people used to say that the Phookas were very numerous in the times long ago; they were wicked-minded, black-looking, bad things, that would come in the form of wild colts with chains hanging around them. The Phookas did great hurt to benighted travellers.'

The Legend of Rathgobáin

O'Curry, the historian, refers to a Gaehilic manuscript of the eighth century now in the Monastery of St. Paul in Carinthia, in which the name 'Gobban Saer' is mentioned in a poem: *Gobban made there, A black conester and a tower'.*

He is also mentioned in *St. Alban's Life,* as being a contemporary of his. As St. Alban lived about the middle of the sixth century, a little more than 150 years before the presumed date of the poem, there is good evidence of the real existence of Gobán Saor as an architect.

The Banshee

Dr. O'Brien in his *Irish Dictionary* writes: 'The *bean-sighe*, woman-fairy, is credulously supposed by the common people to be so affected to certain families that they are heard to sing mournful lamentations about their homes at night, whenever any of the family labours under a sickness which is to end in death. But no families which are not of an ancient and noble stock are believed to be honoured with this fairy privilege.'

In Dingle, the Hussey, Rice and Trant families are said to have their Banshee; in Tipperary, the Butler, Kearney and Keating families.

The Legend of Bottle Hill

The ruins of Mourne Abbey, originally a foundation for Knights Templars, are between the old and new roads from Cork to Mallow.

The Field of Buachalauns

Lady Morgan in her novel *O'Donnell* defines the cluricaune or leprechaun as 'a shrivelled little old man, whose presence marks a spot where hidden treasures lie concealed.'

Teigue of the Lee

Teigue would seem to have belonged to the *feár dearg* fraternity. According to Crofton Croker, the *feár dearg,* the red man, is a member of the fairy tribe in Ireland who resembles Puck or Robin Goodfellow, delighting in mischief or mockery.

During his travels, Crofton Croker actually met the son of the Colonel Pratt mentioned in the story. There were Pratts associated with Beechmount and Gawsworth, two houses in the locality but at a later date.

Hell Hole is well known in Cork. It was, and still is to a lesser degree, a favourite swimming resort on the Lee. It can be a quite sinister-seeming place in some lights and has claimed many a young swimmer's life.

The Legend of the Druid's Daughters

The Milesians are thought to have settled in Ireland about 1000 BC. They were divided into four tribes and the descendants of two of them ruled Munster. Modh Nuaghat was king of Munster at the end of the second century AD, and his great-grandson was Fiacha Muilleathan, which places the time of the story as the third or fourth century. Fiacha was the ancestor of the MacCarthys. The O'Briens are descended from another grandson of Modh Nuaghat, Cormac Cas.

Irish Phrases

a chailín	girleen, my girl
a chroí	my dear, dearest
a chuid	darling
a ghile	dearest
a ghrá gheal	my beloved (my fair love)
a leanbh, a leinbhín	my child, my little child
a mháthairín	my little mother
a mhic, mo chroí	son of my heart
a mhúirnín	darling
a Rí	king
a stór	my dear
a thíghearna	master.
bohereen	*bóithrín,* a little road
buachalaun	the weed ragwort
camán	hurley (hurling)
cannavaun	*canach bán,* bog-cotton
caoine	a wild song of lamentation
cluricaune	leprechaun
Cnocan na Biolaraighe	Watergrasshill, a village
liosanna	ring (fairy) forts
mo mhúirnín	my darling (mavourneen)
míle murdar	a thousand murders
piggin	small cup
Poll na gCat	cave of the cat
potheen	illicitly distilled whiskey
ruaille buaille	hurly-burly
sceachóirí	haws, hawthorn berries
scrid	a rag
shebeen	unlicensed house selling drink
sídhe	*slua sídhe,* the fairy host
sodar	state
Tír na h-Óg	land of youth
tocht	heaviness
ullagone	*olagón,* moaning in sorrow

Legends
of
Kerry

Kerry, one of the most beautiful regions in the
country, inhabited by people with a rare gift for
a colourful turn of phrase, has its own
distinctive legends. Many of them were
recorded in the first half of the nineteenth
century by Thomas Crofton Croker, a
Corkman who went to live in London but who
never lost his interest in the folk tales of the
Irish countryside.

In *Legends of Kerry*, Kerryman Sigerson
Clifford, noted Irish poet, folklorist and
storyteller, retells many of the Crofton Croker
stories and adds a few of his own to make a
collection that spins a magic charm around
some of Ireland's most famous beauty spots —
Killarney, Muckross Abbey, Ross Castle, the
mountains of Mangerton, Torc waterfall,
Innisfallen, Ballinskelligs....